insight text guide

Sue Sherman

The Erratics

Vicki Laveau-Harvie

First published in 2021, reprinted in 2023.

Insight Publications Pty Ltd
3/350 Charman Road
Cheltenham VIC 3192
Australia
Tel: +61 3 8571 4950
Fax: +61 3 8571 0257
Email: books@insightpublications.com.au

www.insightpublications.com.au

A catalogue record for this book is available from the National Library of Australia

Vicki Laveau-Harvie's The Erratics / Sue Sherman

Sue Sherman asserts the moral right to be identified as the author of this work.

ISBNs:
9781922378163 (print)
9781922378170 (digital)
9781922378187 (bundle: print + digital)

Cover design by Gisela Beer

Printed by Markono Print Media Pte Ltd

contents

CHARACTER MAP

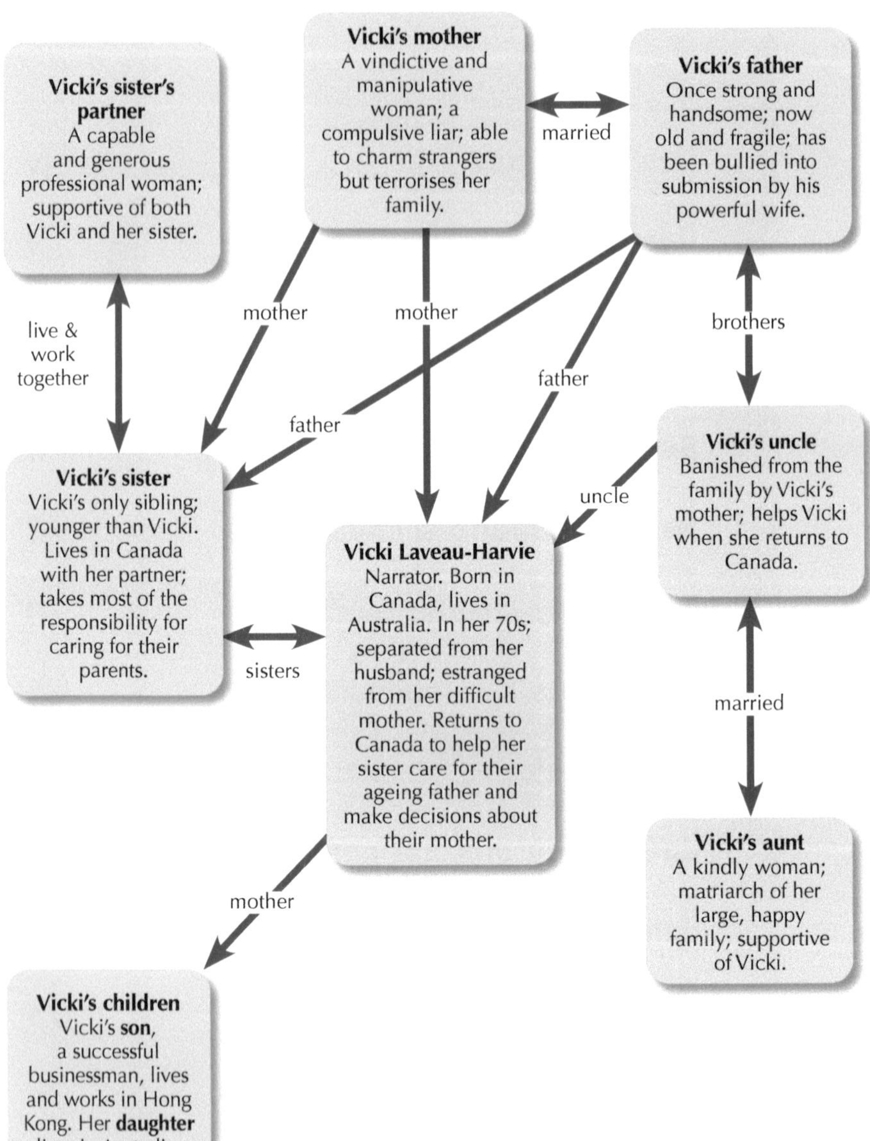

OVERVIEW

About the author

Vicki Laveau-Harvie was born in Canada but lived for many years in France, where she worked as a translator and editor, before settling in Australia, where she lectured in French studies at Macquarie University. After retiring, Laveau-Harvie taught ethics in a primary school.

Laveau-Harvie's memoir *The Erratics* was an unexpectedly successful debut by a writer in her mid-seventies, and won the 2019 Stella Prize for the best book by an Australian woman published in the preceding year. Laveau-Harvie wrote her first draft in 2014, then put it away in a drawer for two years. She brought it out for a Memoir Focus Week at the Varuna Writers' Retreat in the Blue Mountains in November 2016, and subsequently entered the manuscript in the Finch Memoir Prize, which it won. When Finch Publishing closed in December 2018, *The Erratics* was left without a publisher, but after the book was longlisted for the Stella it was acquired by Fourth Estate. Since the Stella announcement, *The Erratics* has maintained a place on the Australian nonfiction bestseller list and international rights to the book have been sold in the US and Canada.

Synopsis

When Vicki's bitter and vindictive mother is admitted to hospital with a broken hip, her frail, forgetful father is left alone in his house and this, after a separation of eighteen years, forces Vicki and her sister to reconnect with their parents. The memoir recounts the efforts of the sisters to prevent their 'mad as a meat-axe' mother (p.1) from ever returning home, where she has been slowly starving their father to death. Burdened by the guilt of having previously left her sister with sole responsibility for their parents, Vicki seeks to make amends.

In sharing the emotional and physical burden of caring for their father, Vicki and her sister's relationship is tested and strengthened. Vicki also observes their father's steady decline, often with wry humour, but always with tenderness and compassion. Their father is completely subjugated to his wife's tyranny, but he is also enthralled by her charisma. After their mother is institutionalised, Vicki and her sister persuade their father to move into a comfortable aged-care facility and their mother dies suddenly of a heart attack. This is a poignant and honest account of a family in crisis which – in the end – is quietly uplifting.

Character summaries

Vicki Laveau-Harvie

Vicki, a middle-aged Canadian woman, lives in Australia. She had fled Canada to escape her vindictive mother who is now in her nineties. Concerned for her father's wellbeing, Vicki returns to Canada when her mother is hospitalised with a broken hip, and many painful childhood memories come flooding back.

Vicki's mother

A cruel and neglectful parent, Vicki's mother also thoroughly intimidates her husband who she is slowly starving. Gifted with a charismatic personality, she beguiles people into believing hurtful lies about her daughters, and creates fantasies about her glamorous life.

Vicki's father

Once strong, handsome and adventurous, Vicki's father is now mentally and physically fragile and cannot care for himself. Vicki and her sister employ full-time carers and he eventually moves into an aged-care facility.

Vicki's sister

Five years younger than Vicki, and living in Canada, Vicki's sister carries most of the responsibility for their ageing parents and sometimes feels resentful. She and her partner are medical professionals and run their own business.

Vicki's sister's partner

Her relationship with Vicki's sister is professional as well as personal. She is a competent and caring woman who is fully supportive of Vicki's sister's commitment to her parents.

Vicki's uncle

Vicki's father's brother – his 'sole surviving sibling' (p.79) – is cast out of the family by Vicki's mother for allegedly ruining her wedding by leaving the rings in the vestry, causing a 'delay of maybe thirty seconds' (p.88). He and his wife are 'king' and 'queen' (p.86) of a large and happy family.

Vicki's son

Vicki's son lives in Hong Kong and operates a successful business as an events organiser. He reassures Vicki that, despite her unfortunate genetic inheritance, she is 'a good person' (p.71).

The 'former downhill skier'

One of a series of highly unsuitable carers employed to look after Vicki's father, she is the only one Vicki and her sister feel – at least for a time – that they can trust (p.140). However, when she takes control of their father's life, Vicki's sister steps in and the carer packs her bags and leaves.

Gerta

An emigrant from Europe, Gerta lives in the same aged-care complex as Vicki's father. Like his wife, she is a 'tough and reliably critical woman' and she 'fills a void' in his life' (p.189).

BACKGROUND & CONTEXT

Geographical setting

Alberta, in Western Canada, is the fourth most populous Canadian province. In the coldest winter months, daytime temperatures range between -15°C and -5°C, but at night can drop as low as -40°C, with glaciers forming in the Rocky Mountain Parks. In her Stella Prize interview (2019), Laveau-Harvie explains that these mountains and foothills are 'practically a character in the book' and she reads a passage that emphasises the landscape's comforting presence:

> When winter comes, summer is the memory that keeps people going, the remembrance of the long slanting dusk, peonies massed along the path, blossoms as big as balloons, crimson satin petals deepening to the black of dried blood in the waning light, deer on the lawns, stock still. (p.4)

Laveau-Harvie's personification of the Rockies also gives them a 'stern and inscrutable face' (p.2). In the winter, the landscape is covered by 'a blinding swathe of white that will mask its disgrace' (p.7). In spring, the mountain peaks lead to the coast where the delta is 'laid out flat, shining like silver and going, Yo, hey, look at me all temperate and fertile, you can even grow fruit here' (p.123). The Rocky Mountains are a dominating physical and psychological presence in Vicki's life.

In the remote farming community where Vicki's parents live, people 'go to bed when … the sun sets' because 'the distance between you and the one yard-light you can see burning on a property across the valley' is 'immense and poignant' (p.93). Thus, the geographical setting helps to create a strong community spirit, shown in the neighbours' visit to Vicki's father at Christmas time, although they park with their vehicles facing outwards in case 'a quick get-away' is needed (p.55).

Historical setting

First Nations peoples in Alberta (where Vicki's parents live) have a long history, which dates back at least 11 000 years. Prior to the arrival of Europeans in North America, the land provided First Nations peoples with everything they required for their mental, physical, spiritual and emotional wellbeing; in return, they respected and cared for the land. An oral storytelling tradition preserved First Nations people's cultural heritage, which was passed from generation to generation. An example is the story Napi tells the spirit of Vicki's mother at the conclusion of the memoir: a creation myth that emphasises the importance of respectful relationships between nature and humankind.

A French explorer named Jacques Cartier arrived on the east coast of (what is now known as) Canada in 1534. Although Cartier did not find the great quantities of gold he was seeking, he did locate abundant fisheries in the Gulf of Saint Lawrence and the mainland's furs; these were very tempting to Europe's commercial interests. Vicki's mother's closets full of mink furs (pp.45–6) reflect the mass slaughter of mink to satisfy the vanity of wealthy women.

Europeans appeared in greater numbers in the 1750s as the fur trade expanded across western North America, and many trading posts were built in the last quarter of the century for the benefit of missionaries and settlers. In 1870, a ranching economy emerged, and flourished, in southern Alberta. Vicki's parents and their neighbours continue the ranching tradition. The Hudson's Bay Company, a trading business, controlled and governed the population, which consisted of First Nations people, Métis people (of mixed European and indigenous ancestry), and European fur traders.

This 'control and governing' euphemistically glosses over the appropriation of First Nations people's land, the erosion of their culture and the exploitation of the land's natural resources. First Nations peoples were decimated by European diseases and by the near-extinction of the buffalo, their main source of livelihood. They were relocated to reservations, while the financial interests of traders were backed by the Royal Canadian Mounted Police (Mounties), who rigidly enforced Canadian law (Davidson & Smith 2021). Laveau-Harvie's memoir spans the years from the mid-twentieth century to the early twenty-first century, and it seems that the tough pioneering spirit of the early settlers has endured in the current inhabitants of the rugged landscape.

Mental health

Vicki's parents show evidence of suffering from a number of mental health disorders. Her mother displays characteristics of both narcissistic and sadistic personality disorders. Narcissists regard their own interests, opinions and feelings as the only ones that matter. Sadists tend to enjoy inflicting pain, suffering or humiliation on others. Paranoia is evident as well in Vicki's mother's belief that 'the world is out to get her' (p.5).

Dementia is a brain disorder affecting thinking and behaviour, and is more common in the elderly. Symptoms include memory loss, confusion, apathy and withdrawal, personality change, and loss of ability to perform everyday tasks. Also common is an inability to recognise family or friends, often causing fear and anxiety, and the kind of aggressive behaviour exhibited by Vicki's mother. By contrast, her father becomes progressively more confused, forgetful and withdrawn, although a diagnosis of dementia is not mentioned in the text.

GENRE, STRUCTURE & LANGUAGE

Genre

Memoir is similar to autobiography but focuses on a specific topic or period rather than an individual's entire life span. Although classified as nonfiction, *The Erratics* employs many features of narrative fiction, particularly in its poetic language. Laveau-Harvie also invests her characters with considerable psychological depth; however, in contrast to narrative fiction, those characters are depictions of real people participating in events that are also real, so the story must be truthfully told. Laveau-Harvie explains her approach to memoir in the following way:

> I have put myself on the page, the real me, as close as I can get, no makeup, no filters. That is your brief as a memoirist: to tell the truth, clear and unadorned. You say not how you wish it had been, but how it was. (Laveau-Harvie 2019)

The generic features of **magic realism** also appear in the memoir; in the final section, the spirit of Vicki's mother converses with Napi, 'the spirit Wise Man of the Blackfoot people' (p.215). The characteristic elements of this genre include the 'juxtaposition of the realistic and the fantastic or bizarre, skilful time shifts, convoluted and even labyrinthine narratives and plots' and the 'miscellaneous use of dreams, myths and fairy stories' (Cuddon 1999), with the purpose of enabling authors to present a more optimistic alternative to a troubled reality. Laveau-Harvie's magic realism presents her mother in a more favourable light and envisages a possible reconciliation between First Nations peoples and Anglo-European Canadians.

Structure

The complexities of characters and their relationships are reflected in the memoir's tangled, nonlinear structure. Time lines overlap and verb tenses shift between present, past and future perfect ('will have …'), emphasising the intersections between past, present and future. Additionally, the omission of inverted commas (speech/quotation marks) occasionally blurs boundaries between dialogue and Laveau-Harvie's authorial comments, reflecting the blurred boundary between author and character, yet the author is always firmly in control. She reminds readers of this with interventions such as: 'Here we are then, in the back story, a year and a half before my mother collapses' (p.77), or 'we aren't there yet' (p.159).

In Vicki's various trips to and from Canada, a linear time sequence can be plotted. After a hiatus of eighteen years (p.89), she returns for a short visit (Chapters 11–14) when her mother writes and implies that Vicki's father will die soon. Eighteen months later, Vicki visits shortly before Christmas after her mother breaks her hip (Chapters 1–9), and again, in the following northern hemisphere summer (Chapter 21). In Chapter 22 ('one year later'), Vicki makes her 'last trip to the house on the edge of the foothills' (p.169); a few months later, her father moves to Vancouver to live with Vicki's sister and then in the Pacific Peace complex. Vicki's visits to her sister and father are more regular once her father is settled at Pacific Peace (Chapters 24–6).

Seasonal changes create another time line. At the start of *The Erratics* Vicki arrives in the Canadian winter (p.18), but her next visit (after her mother's committal) is in an 'Alberta prairie summer' (p.161). One year later she visits again in the summer, spending 'long sunny days' with her sister and father (p.169), but when her sister is forced to dismiss their father's helper and take him back to Vancouver it is a 'grim' Canadian winter with 'snowfall and blizzard gales over the Rockies' (p.174).

Language

The Stella Prize judges described Laveau-Harvie's language as 'understated' with 'naturalistic' dialogue, 'conveying the deep alienation that can exist in a fractured immediate family' (Judges' Report 2019). Her language can also be intensely poetic, such as in this description of the landscape:

> [The Rockies] shine, lit from behind where the sun has set, the snow covering them opalescent ... as the sapphire heavens deepen, the first star high above shining like a diamond on velvet. (p.31)

Laveau-Harvie's descriptions of domestic settings often reflect the characteristics of those who inhabit them. The ruin and neglect in her parents' house symbolises the emotional damage caused by her mother's destructive presence; Vicki must step carefully around 'pickle jars, cans of tomatoes, boxes of salt and bicarb of soda, and the occasional pot-lid ... marking the spots where someone has tried to glue down the wood inlays that have come unstuck' (p.94). In the bathroom, Vicki notices tiles with gilt flecks 'held to the wall by bandaids of various sizes and types' (p.94).

Figurative language, such as similes and metaphors, is a striking feature of Laveau-Harvie's style. For example, the nurses' heads that 'come forward like turtles'' (a simile, p.19) imply that the nurses make themselves visible to observe something interesting but, otherwise, are often not to be seen. An example of a metaphor is the description of 'sinkholes of simmering resentment' that Vicki worries might develop between her and her sister (p.188). A sinkhole is a deep cavity in the ground, concealed by a thin covering of earth. The merging of 'sinkhole' and 'resentment' accentuates the damage caused by the eruption of suppressed anger.

Laveau-Harvie often uses **humour** to lighten the tone, especially when the situations described are confronting and emotionally charged. Forms of humour in the book include the following.

- **Black humour:** The text often makes a joke of adversity or calamity, sometimes at the expense of the sisters' ageing father. Vicki's reference to the 'bottom-line situation' (p.40) reminds her father about his suppositories. His distressing mental decline can have lighter moments.
- **Humorous exaggeration:** Items at the back of the fridge require 'carbon dating' (p.22).
- **Verbal irony** (saying the direct opposite of what one means): Vicki imagines a series of 'self-help books' written by her mother for parents of problem children, in which Book One might be entitled: '*How to Foster a Healthy Sense of Self in your Children (Not!)*' (p.89). The irony, made explicit by the extra word ('Not!'), gives an edge of bitterness to the humour.
- **Mockery:** The Area Health Coordinator's ignorance of the distinction between 'prostate' (the male reproductive gland) and prostrate (lying down) is mocked when Vicki imagines her father 'reclining in a sunny field' (p.39). As a health worker, the coordinator should know the difference.

There are also many instances of **authorial intervention**, when Laveau-Harvie directly addresses the reader. This narrative feature draws explicit attention to writing as an interaction between author and reader. For example, interrupting a reflection about her mother, Laveau-Harvie asks readers, 'Do you want this digression?' (p.73). These interventions create a connection with readers, encouraging their involvement in the story and reminding them that texts are literary constructs. As a consequence, the memoir becomes a metafictional text as it is writing about writing.

CHAPTER-BY-CHAPTER ANALYSIS

Chapter 1 (pp.1–5)

Summary: *Vicki and her sister visit their ninety-four-year-old mother in hospital, where it becomes clear that their mother's already unbalanced mental state has further deteriorated.*

Vicki's mother seems to be showing signs of dementia but, according to her daughters, has always been 'mad as a meat-axe' (p.1). The lies she tells the nurses about how many children she has are an indication of her complete disregard for the truth.

Despite her frustration with the situation and with her mother's lies and outlandish appearance, Vicki must admit that there is something rather admirably defiant about the 'black fringe and bobbed hair' (p.2).

Key vocabulary

Down-underism, Antipodeanism (p.2): a uniquely Australian expression.

Run the ... gauntlet (p.3): former military punishment whereby offenders were ordered to run between two rows of men who struck them with weapons. It now means undergoing a painful but necessary ordeal.

Q What impressions of the relationship between Vicki and her sister are created in this chapter? Explain your reasoning.

Chapter 2 (pp.7–13)

Summary: *The social worker expresses concern about their mother's difficulty in adjusting. Because of this, and despite Vicki's mother's mental instability, the hospital plans to send her home, where Vicki and her sister fear she will 'kill' their father (p.10).*

Preparing for a meeting with hospital staff, Vicki and her sister devise a strategy which they rehearse to ensure their mother is not sent home. During the meeting, the social worker asks leading questions but, instead of criticising her mother, Vicki acknowledges her gifts of 'music, literature, languages' (p.12).

Key point

Laveau-Harvie's descriptions of the Rockies often give them a menacing presence that symbolises her mother's malevolence. Other images of violence, destruction and death in this chapter emphasise the danger of her mother's return home.

Key vocabulary

DVT (deep vein thrombosis) (p.12): a blood clot, generally found in the leg; can travel to the lungs and prove fatal.

Get a bead on (p.8): line someone up in the sights of a firearm; metaphorically, focus attention on someone in order to confront them.

In Cold Blood (p.8): a nonfiction novel by Truman Capote about the brutal murders of a wealthy farming family in Kansas.

Malaise (p.7): general sense of unease or unhappiness.

Stockholm Syndrome (p.8): an unusual situation in which a hostage begins to identify with and form a bond with their captor, as in the case of Patty Hearst, granddaughter of a wealthy American publishing tycoon, who was kidnapped by left-wing terrorists with whom she bonded and joined in a bank robbery.

The Frank slide (p.10): a rockslide in 1903 that buried part of the Canadian mining town of Frank, killing many people.

Vis-à-vis (p.8): the person with whom one is face to face.

Q What does Vicki's sister's exultation (p.9) and her need for 'validation' (p.11) reveal about her relationship with her mother?

Q Does the assumption that a 'suitorless spinster' (p.7) – an older, unmarried woman without a suitor, or partner – would be 'pining' seem like an inappropriate generalisation? Justify your answer.

Chapter 3 (pp.15–20)

Summary: *The story backtracks to Vicki's departure from Sydney. She is met by her sister at Calgary airport and they drive straight to the hospital.*

Laveau-Harvie recounts an episode from her teenage years to highlight her mother's tendency to give others false ideas about her children. Serving afternoon tea to a visitor, Vicki's mother's 'blinding' smile has an edge of hostility, subtly emphasised in the reference to her canines – the four sharp pointed teeth in a human mouth (p.16). She makes a patronising comment that 'Victoire [Vicki] is so fond of Henry James' (p.16), implying that Vicki has sophisticated tastes and reads at an advanced level for her age (fourteen), apparently in an attempt to impress her guest, or perhaps to mock her daughter (or both). This memory is echoed in the scene that concludes the chapter, when Vicki arrives at the hospital ward to discover that she has been falsely described by her mother as a 'famous author'.

Key point

Events in the past and the present overlap and are recounted in the simple present tense, making them seem concurrent. The simultaneous presence of the naive child and the reflective adult narrator sharply contrasts Vicki's childish impressions with her deeper adult understanding of her mother's spite.

Key vocabulary

Ague (p.19): fever.

Berber blend (p.18): carpet made of a combination of wool and nylon.

Bon mot: (p.19): witty remark.

Doppelganger (p.16): spirit or person with an exact resemblance to someone living.

Henry James (p.16): a critically acclaimed American novelist (1843–1916).

Ill hap (p.17): misfortune.

Q What does Vicki's memory of herself at fourteen, sneaking out at night to 'make out' with boys, add to her discussions about memory?

Chapter 4 (pp.21–7)

Summary: *Vicki and her sister take their father and a friend to visit their mother, who puts on an extravagant show of maternal affection and wifely devotion.*

Vicki's mother assigns her visitors roles in her 'little hospital drama' (p.25) while she occupies centre stage, using her personal power and the sheer force of the illusion she has created to hold them all captive – apart from Vicki. Both she and her mother implicitly understand this.

Vicki compares her mother to a 'Ponzi' (p.27): a fraudulent financial investment scheme that pays high returns to existing investors using new investors' money, rather than making real profits, while the directors keep the capital. Likewise, Vicki's mother's creation of 'depth in thin air' lures people to invest in her 'aggrandisement' (p.27), often to their considerable disadvantage.

Key vocabulary

Ashram (p.23): place of religious retreat or seclusion.

Carbon-dating (p.22): method used by scientists to estimate the age of the organic matter found in ancient or prehistoric objects.

Rosary (p.21): prayer ritual of the Catholic religion using a set of beads to count a specific number of prayers.

The chops to trump (p.26): slang expression meaning the ability to outdo or defeat someone.

Q How is Vicki's anger with her mother conveyed in this chapter?

Chapter 5 (pp.29–35)

Summary: *Vicki spends some time with her father; she watches him shuffle across the kitchen and her 'heart cracks' as she remembers him being 'tall and fit and strong' (p.32).*

The phrase 'meanwhile, back at the ranch' (p.29) was a standard subtitle during silent movies, namely Westerns, where a cut from a highly dramatic action scene to something seemingly ordinary 'at the ranch' highlighted the greater importance of the quieter scene. Thus, Vicki's father's heartbreaking 'shuffle' across the kitchen is the real tragedy, unlike her mother's exaggerated 'hospital drama'.

Vicki remembers the very few 'Hallmark moments' (p.32) her family shared. She also remembers drawings at school created by 'crayon scribblings of colour' (p.34) covered by black paint, then the colours were revealed by scratching the surface. Vicki's analogy describes the way people learn about each other and illustrates her own suppressed 'grief' (p.35); the analogy is an example of the inventive figurative language used throughout the memoir.

Key vocabulary

Aurora borealis (p.35): spectacular displays of light in the sky in the northern polar region.

Q What assumptions are made about 'normal' family life, as portrayed on traditional Hallmark greeting cards? What is Vicki's attitude to such families?

Chapter 6 (pp.37–43)

Summary: *Vicki and her sister fill garbage bags with out-of-date medications and the Area Health Coordinator arrives to check on their father.*

The sheer volume of their father's numerous medications suggests the many unpleasant physical effects of ageing, the indignities connected with the failure of bodily functions and the impossibility of his managing his dosages. Yet miraculously, their father has survived – ironically, by forgetting to take most of his pills.

Key point

Towards the end of the chapter, images of regrowth and vitality abound: tiny birds nesting in trees; the snow 'shining like glass' as it melts; and a 'gauzy stratus-cloud arch' blowing in at dawn (p.42). There is a sense of hope in the imagery of renewal suggested by the absence of their mother and the clearing of the house.

Key vocabulary

222s / 292s (p.41): pills for pain relief, once commonly used but now considered dangerous.

Clarion (p.38): a trumpet with a clear, shrill sound, once used in battles.

CWA (p.43): Country Women's Association.

Ergo (p.38): a Latin word meaning 'therefore'.

Pharmacopeia (p.39): collection or stock of drugs.

Prostrate (p.38): lying flat on the ground; the coordinator has confused the word with 'prostate', a gland in the male reproductive system.

Stoner (p.39): (slang) person habitually high on drugs, especially marijuana.

Stools (p.41): medical name for faeces.

Suppositories (p.40): rectal laxatives for relieving constipation.

Vicodin (p.42): an opioid used to treat severe pain.

Wraith (p.39): a ghost or ghostlike image of someone.

Q How well does humour help the sisters cope with their father's physical and mental decline?

Chapter 7 (pp.45–52)

Summary: *The nurses blame Vicki for her mother's unsuitable clothes, unaware that her mother had insisted it was 'hospital garb', and part of the treatment 'protocol' (p.49). In her mother's closets are clothes that have been cut with scissors and look like 'voodoo vestments' (p.50), and an enormous repository of shoeboxes, many filled with hundreds of cancelled cheques.*

When Vicki and her sister were children, their mother would say she would 'get' them and they would not 'even know' she was 'doing it' (p.49). When in this chapter they shop for suitable clothing for their mother, they buy 'jaunty outfits' in colours she will 'hate' (p.51). This is a small but satisfying act of revenge.

Their mother's calculated malice exhibits traits of 'personality disorder' (p.150): she is paranoid, egocentric, sadistic, controlling and a compulsive liar. After finding the cheques in the shoeboxes, Vicki's sister squeezes her hand and they 'stand together … looking out the window' (p.52). It is a silent moment of solidarity which acknowledges the shared traumas of their childhood.

Key vocabulary

Dr Zhivago (p.46): film, set in pre–World War I Russia, where heavy fur coats gave protection from the bitter cold. 'Lara' was the heroine and her theme music became popular in its own right.

Highboy dressers (p.46): tall chests of drawers.

Imelda Marcos (p.52): wife of a former president of the Philippines. During his presidency, she and her husband allegedly stockpiled a multi-billion-dollar fortune, and she owned at least a thousand pairs of designer shoes.

Jaundiced (p.45): cynical.

Sardonic (p.49): mocking or sarcastic.

Q How does the possibility of an undiagnosed mental illness affect the way we view Vicki's mother?

Chapter 8 (pp.53–60)

Summary: *As Christmas approaches, the sisters plan to leave, having organised twenty-four-hour care for their father. Neighbours visit, despite the ill-feeling their mother has generated. When her daughters visit her, she plays the grief-stricken mother, abandoned by her heartless daughters.*

Celebrating the spirit of Christmas, the neighbours arrive at Vicki's parents' house, although parking 'nose-out, ready for a quick get-away' (p.55). The celebration of Christmas reminds Vicki of a different kind of festive season, with 'mangoes and platters of prawns' (p.58), in Australia: that other landscape that has also become her home.

When Vicki and her sister search for Christmas decorations they find none, and Vicki regrets the 'Yule void', seeing it as a denial of 'the deep cultural reasons for festivals' (p.57). As she boards the plane to Hong Kong, Vicki imagines the plane crashing, killing the passengers returning home for Christmas (p.60). The link between family occasions and catastrophe is seemingly embedded in Vicki's subconscious.

Key vocabulary

'Baby, It's Cold Outside' (p.57): popular American song written in 1944.

Lèse-tinsel (p.57): 'lèse' is an obsolete word meaning to lose or discontinue something; here it refers to the absence of tinsel and other Christmas decorations.

Mason–Dixon line (p.57): a line drawn on the US map marking the division between the northern and southern (free and slave, respectively) states, especially during the American Civil War era.

Up the proverbial [creek] (p.55): in a difficult situation.

Yule (p.57): from Old English gēol, meaning 'Christmas'.

Q What is revealed about Vicki's sister by her need to clean a coffee spill on a fellow passenger's coat?

Chapter 9 (pp.61–7)

Summary: *After his Christmas lunch with neighbours, Vicki's father is driven home for a rest. He is awakened by a break-in and presses the alarm on his Supportline bracelet. Vicki decides that neither she nor her sister will fly home to Alberta.*

Hearing a break-in, Vicki's father foolishly prepares to confront the burglars who, fortunately, have fled. Plywood is nailed over the broken windows by the neighbours' boys; police arrive; the neighbours bring leftovers and the 'helper has arrived for her first shift' (p.67). Vicki is reassured that the 'system' they organised has 'worked' (p.67) and is heartened by the neighbours' strong community spirit.

Vicki irritably reflects that if her mother hadn't boasted of their wealth, they would not have been burgled. The incident is reminiscent of the Kansas murders (alluded to on page 8) and is a grim reminder of unseen dangers (also symbolised by the rocks known as the Erratics).

Key vocabulary

Escher (p.62): a twentieth-century Dutch graphic artist. MC Escher is known for disturbing, maze-like pictures of interlocking labyrinths from which there is no escape.

Forensics (p.64): the use of investigative and analytical techniques to collect evidence.

Kafka (p.62): German/Bohemian author whose protagonists are often trapped in disorienting, illogical situations and surreal, nightmarish settings.

Q Why does Vicki feel gratitude towards other people for 'having their own problems' (p.64)?

Q How does Laveau-Harvie convey her concern about the environment, and what are the 'bigger questions' (p.63) implicitly being asked?

Chapter 10 (pp.69–75)

Summary: *Vicki celebrates New Year's Eve in Hong Kong with her son before flying to Sydney. At home, she takes the story back eighteen months, to June, when she received a belated thank-you note from her mother for a Christmas gift, ending with a callous remark, hinting that her father is about to die.*

Vicki needs to 'recover' from her recent contact with her parents in the 'quiet' Sydney suburb where people think she is 'normal' (p.72). Troubling memories, however, remind her that her normality is a facade.

The sisters' offers to support their parents over the years have been met with hostility from their mother and Vicki worries that their browbeaten father might – like the adopted peacock, Peabody – simply choose to die, as the only way in which he can escape from his wife's tyranny.

Key vocabulary

Kalashnikov (p.74): AK-47, a powerful assault rifle used by the military.

Not in Kansas anymore (p.72): a reference to one of Dorothy's lines in the film *The Wizard of Oz*, about suddenly finding oneself in an unfamiliar place.

Q The idea of home is important to Vicki – whether it be Hong Kong, Sydney or Canada. How do these places provide a sense of home for her?

Chapter 11 (pp.77–83)

Summary: *After being warned of her father's imminent demise, Vicki imagines him sitting corpse-like on a ride-on mower, her mother beside him, triumphant over the distress her letter will cause. She calls her father but they both know Vicki's mother is listening. Some months earlier the sisters had called the Mounted Police and asked them to check on their parents, but the officer was informed by Vicki's father that 'those girls are just after the money' (p.79). Eventually, after some unpleasant phone conversations with her mother, Vicki decides to visit her parents.*

Since her previous visit Vicki has spoken to her father only once but, because her mother had picked up the receiver in another room, the conversation was brief and guarded. In Vancouver Vicki stays the night with her sister who, at the last minute, tearfully changes her mind about coming with her to visit their parents (p.82). Her sister's partner later tells Vicki of her sister's fear that Vicki was a 'dead woman walking' (p.83).

The image of a Prairie Gothic painting (p.77) that Vicki carries in her head and the grim reminder of the murderous Norman Bates (in the film *Psycho*) reveal her anxiety over the possibility of her father's imminent demise. Her mother also implies, with calculated spite, that his death would be a consequence of Vicki's wish to see him. Imagery connects Vicki's father's entrapment and torture by his wife with characters in Gothic fiction ('a Prairie Gothic portrait', 'his flesh sinking inward and desiccating like an apple', pp.77–8), and Vicki's sister's fear of going to their parents' house (pp.82–3) suggests that their parents inhabit a Gothic house of horrors.

Key vocabulary

John Deere (p.77): brand name of an American manufacturer of agricultural machinery.

Mona Lisa effect (p.78): reference to the mysterious smile of the subject in Leonardo da Vinci's famous painting.

Norman Bates (p.81): main character in Alfred Hitchcock's 1960 horror film *Psycho*. A serial killer, Bates suffers from psychosis and dissociative identity disorder, believing himself to be his controlling mother.

Prairie Gothic (p.77): reference to the painting *American Gothic* by Grant Wood, depicting a farmer and his daughter (often incorrectly assumed to be his wife) standing in front of a barn.

Pre-emptive karma (p.80): spending one's life doing good in order to avoid unpleasant consequences in one's next existence.

RCMP (p.82): Royal Canadian Mounted Police (also referred to as Mounties).

Q What reasons does Vicki give for visiting her parents (p.82) and how do these reveal her sense of self? Is it a mostly positive or mostly negative self-assessment?

Chapter 12 (pp.85–92)

Summary: *Vicki phones her parents from her uncle and aunt's apartment; her mother insists that Vicki can't stay with 'those people' and demands that she leave immediately (p.87); Vicki's uncle drives her home.*

The conspicuous difference between Vicki's kindly relatives and her uncaring parents emphasises the abnormality of her immediate family. Her aunt and uncle intuitively understand Vicki's embarrassment and tactfully leave the room while she is on the phone.

Vicki agrees to spend the night at her parents'. While supper is cooking her mother vanishes and, when the asparagus starts to burn, Vicki turns off the flame underneath the pot. She searches for her mother, who 'surges silently from a dark doorway' and pushes Vicki violently against the wall – blaming her because the asparagus is 'ruined' (p.90).

Key vocabulary

Cojones (p.92): (colloquial) testicles; symbolic of bravery or heroism.

Cuts a … swathe (p.88): causes substantial damage in a particular place.

The cat's pyjamas (p.91): the best example of its kind.

Q What does Vicki's father's story about his youthful adventures suggest about traditional views of masculinity?

Chapter 13 (pp.93–100)

Summary: *Vicki has a difficult night at her parents'. The bedroom she sleeps in holds unpleasant memories of her visit eighteen years earlier, with her husband and children, when the inadequate sleeping* *arrangements were deliberately unwelcoming. Vicki's father, apparently under instructions from her mother, takes her on a harrowing drive to Shawnessy for lunch.*

During the awkward dinner, Vicki's mother's gushing 'monologue' (p.97) about one of her young piano students is interrupted when the student's mother arrives and informs her of the child's broken arm. Vicki's mother's exaggerated outpouring of grief for her student is an implicit rejection of Vicki's own children and grandchildren whose existence her mother refuses to acknowledge.

Instead of driving to Okotoks (which is close), her father obeys his wife's orders and drives Vicki to Shawnessy, despite his lack of confidence and lack of recent driving experience; this involves the extreme danger of crossing 'three lanes of traffic' with huge trucks 'screaming' (p.99) towards them. Vicki realises that the life-threatening trip is her mother's revenge for her unwelcome visit.

Key vocabulary

Dead Sea Scrolls (p.95): ancient manuscripts, mostly in Hebrew, found in 1947 on the shore of the Dead Sea.

Duke it out (p.96): take part in a physical fight.

Fracas (p.94): chaotic noise or uproar.

Lippizzan dancing horse (p.94): known as 'the dancing white horses of Vienna', they train and perform at Vienna's Spanish Riding School.

Q While enjoying the thrill of adventure as he drives down the highway, Vicki's father disregards the serious risk to his life and his daughter's life. How does Laveau-Harvie's account of this trip shape your response to her father's reckless behaviour?

Chapter 14 (pp.101–8)

Summary: *Vicki's father drives slowly and very erratically, evoking anger from other drivers and endangering his and Vicki's lives. They arrive safely and Vicki asks her uncle to join them for lunch.*

There is nowhere worthwhile to eat in Shawnessy. Vicki's father and uncle are uneasy with each other and relieved when Vicki finishes her coffee; yet her uncle's 'miles behind the wheel', her sister's 'anguish' and her mother's fury don't matter because she has been able to see her father (p.104).

When Vicki leaves the diner with her uncle, she knows that her father will suffer her mother's wrath when he makes it home, and she understands that her father cannot see her again before she returns to Australia. She also recognises his commitment to her mother and his willingness to endure her malevolence.

Key vocabulary

Doppler effect (p.102): increase (or decrease) in the frequency of sound, light, or other waves as the source and observer move towards (or away from) each other.

Fangio (p.102): Argentine racing car driver who won the World Drivers' Championship five times in the 1950s.

Kaffeeklatsch (p.104): informal social gathering for coffee and conversation.

Q Why is it so important to Vicki to discover if there is 'a spark of family feeling' (p.103) between her father and his brother?

Chapter 15 (pp.109–16)

Summary: *Vicki's father is being starved by her mother, who obsesses over his sleep apnoea. Vicki's mother has paid 'gobsmacking' (p.112) amounts of money to scammers on the internet, 'spending big, just because she could' (p.113).*

Vicki's parents' banker makes an appointment to visit them, and when the worried banker reveals the extent of Vicki's mother's expenditure, Vicki's father imagines his 'hard-earned assets ... dissolving in an acid bath', and 'rancour blossoms in his heart' (p.114). Ironically, the banker's visit intensifies her mother's 'mail campaign' (p.114).

Key point

Vicki remembers a little cartoon figure in the newspaper, whose narrow focus on the beauty of the Rockies ignored the dangers in the wider world. Her mother's focus on the world is similarly narrow: reading the newspaper, she sees only 'a gallery of horrors' (p.115), and subjects her family to daily stories of carnage and death.

Key vocabulary

Group of Seven (p.113): group of seven highly regarded Canadian landscape painters.

Sleep apnoea (p.110): temporary cessation of breathing during sleep, sometimes causing death.

Q Why might Vicki's father feel anger and bitterness over his wife's extravagant spending but not over her mistreatment of their daughters?

Chapter 16 (pp.117–23)

Summary: *At the airport, Vicki gazes at the statue of Sam Livingston, honouring his impressive achievements. Flying over the Rockies, Vicki envisages her plane plummeting into the chasms below, and the passengers, who will 'disappear' into the 'gigantic mineral presence', would be 'no more' (p.119).*

Sam Livingston's statue ensures he will always be remembered, unlike the passengers in the plane – of whom there would be 'no trace' if the plane crashed (p.119). Vicki sees her early life as being like 'the blank bit that airplanes routinely plummet through'; it is 'not merely faded ... It's not there' (p.120).

Vicki is grateful for blankness. She had shaken herself 'free' and fled to 'far-flung places' where she felt 'safe', unlike her sister who 'feels the blows of the past continuously in her present' (p.120). The price to be paid for Vicki's freedom is her lingering guilt.

Q What evidence – if any – does the text show of her sister's anger at Vicki? Is her anger justified? Explain your reasoning.

Key vocabulary

Audrey Hepburn, Lauren Bacall (p.121): glamorous Hollywood actresses of the 1950s.

Cree children (p.121): descendants of one of the largest groups of First Nations peoples in North America.

Pre-Raphaelite (p.121): the Pre-Raphaelites were a group of artists working in London in the 1840s; their paintings are known for portrayals of young women with long wavy hair, often threaded with flowers.

Proust's madeleine tea-cake (p.120): reference to an early-twentieth-century novel by Marcel Proust, whose narrator eats the crumbs of a madeleine cake dipped in tea and suddenly remembers many details of his past.

Stetsons (p.121): wide-brimmed hats, traditionally worn by American cowboys.

Q Does Laveau-Harvie suggest it is better to remember or forget the past? Explain your reasoning.

Chapter 17 (pp.125–31)

Summary: *The 'watershed affair' (p.125) of her mother's broken hip evokes two upsetting memories for Vicki: firstly, at eight, babysitting her three-year-old sister; and secondly, the phone call from an old friend offering condolences for her mother's alleged death.*

Vicki remembers an event when, before leaving her children alone in the house at night, Vicki's mother warned them about evil strangers intending harm and knocking on the door. When an 'unidentified man' knocks, Vicki pulls her sister into the shadows, but her sister rushes forward, shouting at the stranger to 'go away' (p.129).

As adults, Vicki and her sister's dealings with their mother echo their childhood responses to danger: Vicki retreats while her sister 'stands her ground' (p.129), to the detriment of both sisters. Vicki later comes to understand the traumatic babysitting incident as an example of how the 'lava of lunacy can pervade a life' (p.127).

Key vocabulary

Bumptious (p.127): annoyingly self-assertive.

High moral dudgeon (p.127): anger and resentment.

Hubris (p.128): excessive pride often leading to a downfall.

Watershed affair (p.125): turning point.

Q To what extent is it possible to feel pity for this 'bitterly unhappy and vindictive old woman' (p.126)?

Chapter 18 (pp.133–41)

Summary: *A small 'window of opportunity' (p.134) exists for the sisters to prevent their mother from returning home and 'killing' (p.135) their father; they organise carers for him, who, apart from a former downhill skier, prove to be highly unsuitable.*

When the downhill skier takes Vicki's father to visit his wife in hospital, his wife abuses him and attacks his carer with her cane. In the car, the 'compassionate girl' sits with him while he 'weeps' (p.140). It is the last time he visits his wife.

Vicki hopes the 'gulf' already separating her sister and herself will not be filled with 'seething resentment' when she is on her 'far away island continent ... gnawed by guilt' (p.136). Although their experiences differ, Vicki's burden is no less difficult than her sister's.

Key vocabulary

Obsequious (p.138): using insincere flattery, hoping to benefit oneself.

Thrice-bedamned (p.135): an allusion to Milton's long poem *Paradise Lost*. 'Accursed Devil, thrice damned is all thy race' is the curse God places on the serpent in the Garden of Eden. The allusion mocks Vicki's mother's self-importance.

Q Given her mother's cruelty, why might Vicki feel sympathy for the 'pain' (p.134) and 'despair' (p.135) her mother will endure when she realises she will not be going home?

Chapter 19 (pp.143–51)

Summary: *Vicki's sister and her partner leave for their annual holiday on a Hawaiian island, and Vicki manages their parents' affairs by phone and email from Australia. She talks to her mother's doctor and regularly calls her father as well as her aunt and uncle.*

Her mother's doctor orders a 'psychological competency test', which might result in her mother being declared competent and sent home (p.145). The psychiatrist's report states that Vicki's mother possibly has a 'full-blown personality disorder' (p.150) but avoids declaring her either competent or incompetent.

Vicki feels 'mostly sad' that her mother has 'slipped up' by failing to create a more believable 'fantasy' than the one about saving the 'old Jews' (p.149). Despite her mother's malice, Vicki admires her determination to avoid confinement in an institution.

Key vocabulary

Boondocks (p.147): colloquial term for remote and backward rural areas.

Kvetching (p.148): Yiddish word meaning complaining.

Q What is revealed about Vicki by the objects she salvages from her parents' house?

Chapter 20 (pp.153–9)

Summary: *Vicki's mother is admitted to the dementia ward; Vicki's father suffers heart failure and spends two weeks in hospital.*

The hospital team decides Vicki's mother is 'competent' and can be discharged (p.154). Vicki's sister insists that their mother's case be reconsidered, and a second report declares her mentally incompetent. Vicki's sister gleefully sings 'something about the wicked witch being dead' when telling Vicki of her mother's fate but Vicki feels 'only grief' (p.157). She thinks of the things her mother 'will never see again, the ... Rockies from the windows of her house', and all 'the things she found beautiful and bought and ... hoarded' (p.157).

After 'Nuclear Thursday' (Vicki's father's devastating hospital visit to his wife), Vicki's father is admitted to hospital with 'congestive heart failure', which is an indication of how very 'badly he is hurt', both physically and emotionally; his heart is finally 'broken' (p.156). Their mother's capacity for destruction is frightening.

Key vocabulary

'Ding-Dong! The Witch is Dead' (p.157): song from the film *The Wizard of Oz*; Vicki's sister associates their mother with the wicked witch from that story.

Q What is Laveau-Harvie's view of the care of the elderly (pp.154–5)? Find other examples to support your opinion.

Chapter 21 (pp.161–7)

Summary: *Vicki and her sister attend a 'compulsory' (p.162) meeting at the hospital which their mother also attends; their mother declares that she never again wants visits from the family. Vicki, her sister and her sister's partner carry out maintenance work at their parents' property.*

After the disastrous hospital meeting, Vicki's sister agrees with the chaplain that her mother will 'come around' and promises that they will be there when she does (p.164). Vicki is amazed because her 'dearest wish' (and her sister's, she thinks), is that her mother, wearing her expensive stiletto heels, will slip on the 'recently mopped' hospital floor and die (p.165).

Vicki describes her father's 'man gear' dangling above her sister's head as she tries to unplug the drain as he is showering, and Vicki is appalled at this unwanted 'level of intimacy' (p.166). Beneath the humorous tone, however, there is also pathos in their father's reversion to a level of childhood indifference to his nakedness.

Key vocabulary

Bally pumps (p.162): designer high-heeled shoes.

Exegesis (p.163): explanation or interpretation.

Ingratiate (p.164): attempt to please and get approval from others.

Q How does Laveau-Harvie convey the effects of their mother's behaviour at the hospital on Vicki and her sister?

Chapter 22 (pp.169–76)

Summary: *Vicki makes her final visit to her parents' house. She and her sister are uneasy about the downhill skier, who has become possessive of their father.*

Driving towards the Rockies, Vicki observes the dying fir trees: they are 'victims of the Japanese beetle', an insect that is unable to survive extreme cold but has been able to survive in a warmer winter and thus damage the trees (p.170). A parallel between destructive forces in nature and conflict in families suggests that there is a pivot point (such as 'Nuclear Thursday', p.155) where relationships become unsustainable.

Vicki's sister pressures the downhill skier into leaving, and suggests that her father move to the coast to be near her. He agrees and leaves with the cat, relieved that he will not have to look at the chandelier (a reminder of his wife) any more.

Key vocabulary

Dour Glaswegian (p.172): solemn or gloomy person from Glasgow, a major city in Scotland.

Kleptomaniac (p.175): someone with an uncontrollable impulse to steal.

Q How important is the role of Vicki's sister's partner in Laveau-Harvie's exploration of family relationships?

Chapter 23 (pp.177–83)

Summary: *Vicki's sister, with her partner and some friends, moves into her parents' house and together they clear it out so it will be rentable. When people arrive for the auction of the contents, Vicki imagines a flock of vultures picking over a carcass.*

Vicki refuses her sister's request to help with clearing out their parents' house, saying she is 'still working', but the real reason is more complicated (p.178). She recognises her sister's enthusiasm for a 'challenge' but also perhaps her need to dismantle 'a past that haunts her' (p.178). Vicki is also daunted by the possibility of hidden dangers in the bomb shelter.

Vicki's response is reminiscent of her fearful response to the stranger at the door when they were children (recounted on page 129). Ironically, in this instance, Vicki's fear proves a wiser option than her sister's 'determination to get things done' (p.129). Her sister's exposure to toxins, combined with 'fatigue and stress' (p.179), probably causes her near-fatal illness.

Key vocabulary

Angioedema (p.179): rapid swelling of the area beneath the skin. It is normally an allergic reaction.

Q In view of Vicki's unhappy experiences in her parents' house, why might she find reading the sale catalogue of its contents so heartbreaking?

Chapter 24 (pp.185–92)

Summary: *Before taking their annual holiday, Vicki's sister and her partner find temporary accommodation for her father in a comfortable* *and well-run aged-care facility. There he meets fellow resident Gerta: a 'tough' and 'critical' European woman (p.189). When they return to collect him, he decides to remain where he is. Vicki's sister is rushed to hospital with a breathing obstruction.*

Although Vicki and her sister care about their father, ensuring that he is comfortable and well looked after, Vicki is still somewhat resentful that he 'went along' with their mother in 'disinheriting' them (p.187). Vicki also imagines 'sinkholes of simmering resentment' (p.188) in her sister because of Vicki's lesser commitment to their father's care.

His daughters conclude that his affinity with Gerta fills a 'space reserved for a carping, deluded woman who will endlessly remind him to be wary of everyone around him' (p.189).

Key vocabulary

Gina Rinehart (p.186): wealthy chair of Hancock Prospecting, a privately-owned Australian mining company founded by her father.

RV (p.186): recreational vehicle, such as a camper van, with living accommodation for holiday trips.

Third-age complex (p.188): residential care facility for the elderly.

Q What values does Vicki's sister identify with by insisting that she is 'working class' (p.186)?

Chapter 25 (pp.193–200)

Summary: *In the emergency department, nobody knows what is wrong with Vicki's sister and she almost dies. She improves and is sent home 'hyped-up' on steroids (p.195), where she rages at her partner and Vicki. Something in their father's brain has 'snapped' and his grip on reality dissolves (p.198).*

Vicki's father recounts stories of his adventurous past which may or may not be true. One story involves a woman who 'backed away' when she saw the size of his penis (p.199). Such disinhibition is often due to increasing cognitive difficulties of the kind later described to the sisters by the director of the care home (p.205).

In the car, Vicki and her sister laugh at their father's story about his impressive sexual appendage 'until the tears run down [their] faces' and continue 'for quite some time' (p.200). Their laughter has also released pent-up tears of sorrow for their father's sad decline.

Key vocabulary

Damsels (p.198): old-fashioned literary term for young women needing to be rescued from danger by handsome young heroes.

Derring-do (p.198): display of courage or heroism.

Q What role does humour play in this chapter?

Chapter 26 (pp.201–8)

Summary: *As an experienced medical professional, Vicki's sister is unsettled by being 'just another patient' (p.201). She believes her illness was caused by exposure to toxins while cleaning the family home. When their father's health declines he is moved into a 'higher-care' option which is 'the last stop before the end of the line' (p.205).*

The health of Vicki's father's old cat deteriorates and he agrees that the cat should be taken to the vet. For Vicki, this is a sombre reminder that her father's 'standard of care will decline gradually and drastically' (pp.205–6).

Without the cat, their father becomes listless and her sister finds a replacement cat at the animal rescue shelter; although this cheers her father, Vicki knows he can feel 'the downward slide' (p.206).

Key vocabulary

Acronyms (p.202): words formed from the first letters of other words (e.g. a SIM card is a Subscriber Identification Module).

Q Comment on the metaphor of the train journey (p.205). Does it present a (nihilistic) view of life as ultimately meaningless? Or is it more positive? Explain your answer.

Chapter 27 (pp.209–17)

Summary: *Their mother's sudden death takes them all by surprise: she goes peacefully in her sleep.*

After Vicki receives a condolence email, she and her sister agree to inform their father before someone else does. He 'smiles sadly', describing their mother as a 'nice gal' (p.213). Thinking of her own decline, Vicki imagines an alien future world where people receive emails on implanted contact lenses, and where Canada has been wiped off the map by a US 'readjustment' of boundaries, and she decides that living in the kind of mental 'fog' that surrounds her father would be a better option (p.214).

Key point

The appearance of her mother's spirit with the Blackfoot wise man, Napi (p.215), symbolically draws their two cultures together. She apologises for her hat of 'farmed mink' (p.215), but Napi reminds her that she protected animals on her property. His message about having a 'wider view' and creating more 'scope ... for the good stuff' (p.217) is also part of Laveau-Harvie's message about the importance of the environment.

Key vocabulary

Indomitable (p.209): determined, unable to be defeated.

Rage against the dying of the light (p.210): the refrain and final words from Dylan Thomas' poem 'Do Not Go Gentle Into That Good Night', urging the poet's father to defy death.

Q Does Laveau-Harvie's incorporation of a Blackfoot creation myth seem like cultural appropriation, or is it a respectful acknowledgement of the Blackfoot story? Explain your reasoning.

CHARACTERS & RELATIONSHIPS

Vicki

Key quotes

'I feel transparent, like a wonton wrapper in a steamer basket. The longer I stay, the less real I feel.' (p.45)

'When I could, I took to fleeing ever farther, a moving target working at making herself fainter in the cross-hairs ...' (p.129)

Laveau-Harvie's memoir reveals both her honesty and her courage as she reconstructs her traumatic childhood in her search for the 'truth' (p.12). Young Vicki's sense of self is shaped by the malevolence of her mother who is out to 'get' her (p.49). There are incidents so traumatic that Vicki manages to survive by remembering 'nothing' (p.122). One memory fragment is of her mother suddenly and savagely shearing off her ponytail, with 'sabre-sharp' scissors brushing against her scalp (p.122). It is an incident so terrifying that the aftermath has become a blank but it still makes her sister shudder.

The consequence of her mother's malevolence is that, as an adult, Vicki becomes 'hyper-vigilant ... forever on the lookout for the early warning signs of the ferocity that is in all of us' (p.121). Vicki's vulnerability is deftly captured in the imagery of the wonton wrapper. The delicacy and transparency of the Chinese dumpling suggest the emotional fragility Vicki feels when she returns to Canada.

Family relationships

Plagued by guilt at having fled to Australia, Vicki imagines the anger her sister 'must have felt' (p.123) because of the greater responsibility she carries for their parents. Living in Sydney, Vicki is as far away as possible. When she returns to Canada, tensions arise between Vicki and her sister. Their uncertainty with each other is evident when Vicki's laughter at her sister's seemingly 'funny' comment about her father's medications (p.40) causes unintended offence, and they stare at each other in a 'surprisingly unfriendly fashion' (p.41).

Suddenly, Vicki understands 'those family feuds' in which 'whole generations' do not speak to each other (p.41). Thus, when Vicki needs help, she feels thoroughly undeserving of the kindness of her aunt and uncle, who have also been ostracised by her parents. These generous people demonstrate the strength of family relationships in times of crisis. Likewise, when her parents suddenly deteriorate, Vicki promptly returns home to share the burden with her sister, honouring 'a commitment made absent-mindedly years ago', that she never dreamed 'would be called in' (p.17).

Key point

When her sister angrily points out Vicki's attentiveness to their father, despite what he 'did and didn't do', and alleges that, in comparison, only a brush with death has made her worthy of Vicki's notice, Vicki is dismayed (p.195). Sensing her sister's vulnerability, Vicki reflects that she tried her 'best' (p.196), and her admiration for her sister is clear in her account of her sister facing a pack of angry dogs and rescuing her. Vicki's willingness to admit the element of truth in her sister's allegation shows her commitment to their relationship.

Vicki's mother

Key quotes

'It occurs to me that she is a kind of flesh and blood pyramid scheme, a human Ponzi. You buy in and you are hooked. You have an investment in believing the projections, the evangelical 3D laser image of personal power …' (p.27)

'Your mother cuts a wide swathe of misery where she passes …' (Vicki's uncle, p.88)

Vicki's mother is an accomplished and intelligent woman: she reads widely (p.95); she is fluent in French (p.131) and Spanish (p.95); and she teaches piano (p.97). However, her defining characteristic is her malevolence. The pleasure she derives from inflicting pain is revealed in the 'touch of sadness' she feels because her vulnerable children are not 'more worthy prey' (p.49).

Their mother's random attacks on her family, and on other unwary people, are devastating: she shoves Vicki violently against the wall for ruining the asparagus (p.90) and viciously 'clubs' an 'unsuspecting' librarian who tries to help her (p.112). Her flagrant 'squandering' of her husband's 'hard-earned assets' is an attempt to disempower him (p.114) and increase her own power by spending 'all of her husband's money' in order to 'win her own' (p.111).

Family relationships

At the hospital, her husband's 'mute devotion' as she 'holds the floor, radiating clarity and benevolence', makes him a willing captive to her powerful 'aura' (p.27). Her piteous portrayal of the 'devout mother' (p.26) aligns the sympathetic nurses with her against her seemingly heartless daughters, deliberately making their dealings with hospital staff more difficult. More spitefully, she manages to convince her husband that Vicki and her sister are 'just after [their parents'] money' (p.79), and that they plan to put them both into a nursing home (p.146). This further alienates her husband from his daughters. While Vicki is able to suppress memories of her mother's acts of random cruelty, her sister's relief that 'the wicked witch' is (metaphorically) 'dead' (p.157) reveals the enduring power of her evil presence.

Social interactions

Vicki's mother's interactions with others are characterised by her hostility and dishonesty. Vicki's parents' door is 'open to no one' (p.5) and some of the neighbours 'bear the stamp' of their previous unpleasant interactions with Vicki's mother (p.55). When confronted about her expenditure by the banker, she 'adopts a defensive position of teary ... contrition' and attributes it to the ongoing 'grief' of 'losing her one and only child' (p.113). In hospital, she assumes the piteous persona of a neglected and suffering mother (p.59).

After she is deemed 'mentally incompetent' and 'not free' to leave the hospital to 'go where she will', Vicki's mother refuses to 'give up' (p.156). Unaccustomed to not getting her own way, their mother spends years 'campaigning for her release', writing 'heart-rending letters to people she knew or thought she knew decades earlier ... whom she begs for help' (p.156). As a form of revenge, she refuses to see her family, and 'tries to institute divorce proceedings' (p.156).

Key point

It is an ironic twist of fate that this spiteful woman who denied her husband his freedom is now incarcerated in a locked dementia ward, and it seems as if a kind of moral justice is operating.

The 'eminent psychiatrist' finds that, even though Vicki's mother is aggressive and 'delusional', she is a 'charmer' who is capable of 'coherent and sophisticated thought, logic, and a sense of humour' (p.150). However, she manages to create such 'misery' (p.88) in the lives of other people that her own life ends in 'self-imposed solitude', with only a paid companion at her side (p.210).

Vicki's father

Key quotes

'I love her, he says, darting me a piercing little glance.' (p.33)
'Busy road, he says. Bunch of nuts driving too fast. He pulls himself closer to the steering wheel and floors it.' (p.100)

Vicki's father's character is formed by his values and his achievements. Descended from a 'dour Glaswegian' (p.172), her father has a strong work ethic that allows him to prosper. His successful career provides enough money to fund his wife's 'extravagant' spending and he feels 'a kind of grudging pride' that she has spent lavishly 'just because she could' (p.113). His work ethic dictates his belief that everyone should 'be happy to contribute to the family' (p.127). He is critical of Vicki's request for a reward (a fifteen-cent Dick Tracy comic book) for babysitting her sister, yet he 'pretends not to notice' the demolition of family values by his wife, who is 'punching holes in the bottom of the boat' (p.128).

In his aged-care facility, where he feels the need to reclaim some of his power, his conversations often begin with 'do you have any idea how much I'm worth?' (p.190). He must also remind himself of his sexual power by referring to the size of his penis (p.199). In Canada's capitalist, patriarchal culture, the traditional markers of male power are evident in her father's tales of his youthful adventures (p.198); all that remains in his old age is his financial power, and he proclaims it repeatedly.

Family relationships

Although Vicki's father declares his love for his wife, he also knows that it is not possible for her to come home from hospital because she would 'finish him off' (p.33). Indeed, Vicki reasons, if he didn't love her mother, it wouldn't have been decades since he'd seen his daughters, and nor would he have trouble 'telling his daughters apart' (p.33). He also 'went along' with his wife in 'disinheriting' Vicki and her sister and 'removing any right [they] had to help him in his old age' (p.187). Her father becomes increasingly passive as his mental faculties decline and he retreats into an inner world when he '[turns] off his hearing aid for good' (p.110).

When Vicki returns to Canada after her mother is hospitalised, her father's physical decline is painfully clear: a consequence of systematic starvation by his wife. When Vicki puts her arms around him, she feels 'only bone' (p.90). Vicki and her sister acknowledge their father's passive submission to his wife's schemes, and are aware of the enormous physical and financial danger in which she has been placing him.

Key point

In his youth, Vicki's father revelled in 'excitement, danger and possibilities'. He boasts of a 'miraculous escape', in a plane with a 'mad Australian' – a consequence of sheer audacity and his 'extremely good physics calculations' (pp.91–2). Thus, the frail old man on the road to Shawnessy, who 'floors it' (p.100) and accelerates across three lanes with huge trucks speeding towards him, is still, at heart, the young and invincible daredevil.

Vicki's sister

Key quotes

'I feel she has strained for years, jumping again and again like a terrier, trying to see over the wall of [her parents'] rejection.' (p.17)

'She said that hearing her childhood name cast her back into the black chasms of before and we were not to do it.' (p.23)

Vicki's sister's childhood was dominated by her mother's erratic behaviour. Needing to sever her genetic connection with her mother, she told people she was adopted, because she 'wanted to be adopted' (p.25). As an adult, Vicki's sister gains the kind of control and order in her life that her mother made impossible. As a successful businesswoman, Vicki's sister 'can get things done' (p.129), and quickly takes charge of any situation in which someone is 'unsure how to proceed' (p.175). When her parents' house needs clearing out, she rises to the 'logistical occasion', seeing it as 'a showcase for her formidable organising abilities' (p.178).

When the hospital plans to discharge her mother, Vicki's sister resists their 'best bully tactics' (p.155). She draws on her medical knowledge to dispute her mother's alleged competence and insists that her father's 'shock and despair', and his hospitalisation for heart failure after 'Nuclear Thursday' (p.155), are evidence of the dangers of her mother's release. Although badly shaken after the confrontation, Vicki's sister fulfils her 'mission' (p.156) to prevent her mother from being 'unleashed onto the unsuspecting world outside' (p.154).

Family relationships

Vicki's sister accepts her duty to look after her parents in their old age, and calls on Vicki to honour a promise that she would help (p.17). Over the years, Vicki's sister has made repeated attempts to 'reach out and connect' with her parents but has been 'beaten back' (p.82). She plans to accompany Vicki on a visit to her parents but – at the last minute – can't go through with it. Bursting into tears at the airport, she hugs Vicki as if she 'was going to war' and she might 'never see [her] again' (p.83).

She warns Vicki that their parents hate them and, according to her mother, believe they are 'just after the money' (p.79). Her sister is so hurt by this accusation that she rings her uncle, wondering if she is, unknowingly, so 'venal and horrible' that her mother's 'pronouncement' might be 'true' (p.79). Beneath her capable and efficient exterior, Vicki's sister is a vulnerable woman whose mother's cruelty and parents' rejection has eroded her self-esteem.

Key point

Vicki remembers childhood paintings created by scratching black surfaces with a sharp point to reveal hidden colours. She warns that you 'scratch' her sister 'at your peril' because her memories erupt like a 'geyser of ... black and viscous' rage (p.35). The traumatic memories that her sister carries make Vicki 'glad' that she is able to forget parts of the past (p.123).

Vicki's sister's partner

Key quote

'My sister's partner is a handy person and wishes to inspect the elevator doors to see if there is any way to rig them to open onto a void when [Vicki's] mother pushes the button.' (p.155)

When Vicki and her sister drive to Okotoks to clean their parents' house, her sister's partner remains at home to 'run their business by herself' (p.18). When accompanying Vicki and her sister on a subsequent visit, she impresses Vicki with her 'can-do spirit' (p.165). Following Vicki's sister's dramatic collapse, her partner, a 'medical person herself', deals 'quietly but with some urgency' with the staff at the hospital as the equipment monitoring Vicki's sister's heart rate shows how close she is to 'not making it' (p.194). Her ability to remain calm and in control during a crisis is admirable and, although mostly a background presence, she is a thoroughly dependable presence in Vicki's sister's life.

After Vicki's sister learns of the attempted burglary at her father's house, her partner 'looks grimly at the placemat in front of her, already set for tomorrow's breakfast', thinking she will again be left to run the business while Vicki's sister 'flies to the rescue' (p.67). It is clear that Vicki's parents' problems sometimes make life hard for her sister's partner, yet both women are strengthened by their loving and supportive relationship.

Vicki's son

Key quote

'With your family history ... with your parents – if nurture calls the shots, logically you should be a serial killer.' (to Vicki, p.71)

In Hong Kong on New Year's Eve, Vicki's son is responsible for the fireworks extravaganza: 'festivities for the privileged', among whom he moves 'with aplomb' (p.70). Vicki watches her son fondly, 'threading his way through party people ... shaking hands and kissing girls' (p.71). She is heartened by his reassurance that – despite her parents – she is a 'good person ... triple-plated' (p.71).

Her son's limited contact with his grandparents consists of a visit 'eighteen years ago', when their grandmother made it clear that they were unwelcome (p.95). His concern for his mother convinces him that she should not 'go to Canada any more' because it makes her 'sad' (p.71).

Vicki's aunt and uncle

Key quote

'They act like family. They are family.' (p.82)

Seeing them from a distance at the airport, Vicki is not sure her aunt and uncle will recognise her but they hurry forward and warmly embrace her (p.83). Vicki also remembers their kindness to her sister after the 'RCMP intervention fiasco' (p.82). Their warmth and generosity contrast markedly with the hostility of her mother, whose angry voice 'comes burning white-hot down the phone lines', ordering her not to stay with 'those people' (p.87). Vicki's anxiety over the tightness in her father's voice when he rings and begs her to come home rather than stay with her uncle and aunt (p.87) sends her uncle on the long drive to her parents' house, despite the many miles he has already driven that day (p.88).

Although they have suffered grief, Vicki's uncle and aunt can 'smile at the fullness of their life' (p.86). With their many children, grandchildren and great-grandchildren, they embody the spirit of family togetherness. Their daughter, Vicki's cousin, drives from Montana to see Vicki, and she and her parents spend a day driving her around the little towns of her childhood. The notion that 'blood calls to blood' (p.17) is manifest in this family, which nurtures Vicki and protects her.

The 'former downhill skier'

Key quote

'But the one who will do us in is the one we trust the most, the big young former downhill skier who dealt with the fridge. She seems capable.' (p.140)

The downhill skier 'pitches in bravely' (p.22) as Vicki and her sister tackle the chaos of their parents' house. Her sense of humour lightens the mood as she draws on archaeological and scientific imagery to describe the contents of the fridge: items at the back of the fridge require 'carbon dating', and she jokes that the 'delicatessen period' mayonnaise could produce penicillin (p.22). She also seems genuinely fond of their father, taking him out to lunch and to see the animals on her property (p.140).

Although thoughtful and 'compassionate' (p.140), the carer whom Vicki and her sister trust resigns from the agency and moves in with Vicki's father, deciding she is the only one who has his 'best interests at heart' and that his daughters 'do not care' (p.174). While her intentions might be good, she oversteps a professional boundary and is promptly fired by Vicki's sister (p.175).

Gerta

Key quote

'She is a tough and reliably critical woman given to believing the worst about everything and everyone ...' (p.189)

Gerta is the only resident at the Pacific Peace third-age complex their father will 'tolerate' (p.189). According to rumour, she is there 'under severe duress' and with her 'carping' and delusions she 'fills a void' created by the absence of his wife (p.189). She is also – apart from Vicki – one of only two people in the memoir to be named, the other being Felicity (p.189), the director of Pacific Peace; the latter highlights an ironic mismatch between a name meaning happiness and Felicity's constant 'ire' (anger) over the creatures brought by Gerta's cat into the foyer.

Gerta is both 'protective' of Vicki's father (unlike his wife) and 'abrasive', and her father's attraction to her leads Vicki to 'marvel at the complexities of the human heart' (p.190).

THEMES, IDEAS & VALUES

Identity

Key quote

'I am at home in the fog. I have several names … and I negotiate the fog under cover of one or the other. I don't answer to any of them.' (p.15)

At a basic level, a person's name is integral to their sense of identity. Vicki's middle name, 'Victoire', is designed 'to impress' (p.16), and to affirm her mother's sense of her social and intellectual superiority. Vicki redefines her identity by altering her name, dropping her third name which she finds 'twee' (p.16) and inconvenient, as her full name is too long for the available space on official forms. Her sister also changes her name because 'her childhood name cast her back into the black chasms of before' (p.23). By altering their birth names, both sisters symbolically sever, or at least weaken, their connection with their mother, and as a child Vicki's sister had expressed a strong wish for having been 'adopted' (p.25).

Their father also attempts to erase his connection with his wife by claiming to have adopted daughters who are 'nothing to do with her' (p.25). In redefining his wife as a 'seriously flawed childcare choice', Vicki believes that he aims to revoke her mother's power over him and to reclaim his banished daughters (p.25). His ability to 'live with' (p.25) this conception of their mother suggests that his self-image has been strengthened by his attempt at erasing his wife. Turning off his hearing aid 'for good' (p.110) is also a way of escaping her 'brain-washing' (p.10)

Vicki's escape to 'far-flung places' (p.120) is an attempt to assert her individuality and independence from her oppressive mother. In connecting herself with a culture in which 'mangoes and platters of prawns and lychees' are essential to the Christmas tradition (p.58), she also redefines her cultural identity. The identities the characters assume at different stages in their lives reflect their values and are often connected with a need for survival.

Key point

One of the memoir's most noticeable features is the absence of almost everyone's names, apart from Vicki's. Her parents and sister are identified by their familial relationships. Other people are defined by their status as family friend, neighbour or acquaintance, or by their connection with Vicki's parents as medical professionals, advisors or paid carers. The namelessness of these people limits their identities to their connection with Vicki's family as participants in its saga of troubles.

Gender identity

Aged ninety-four, and still capable of 'carrying ... off' her 'black fringe and bobbed hair' (p.2), Vicki's mother conforms to stereotyped gender expectations requiring women to maintain a youthful and glamorous appearance – an appearance which, in patriarchal societies, is subjected to a judgemental male gaze. She shows her feminine credentials (and elevated social status) by wearing expensive designer clothes and dangerously high stiletto heels. She also takes 'double doses, or perhaps triple, of ... thyroid medication' to appear fashionably 'emaciated' (p.110).

Although Vicki's mother's pursuit of her own power and wealth might seem like a challenge to gender stereotypes, she is more motivated by her sense of her own superiority than by any concern for the necessity of social change for women. More effective in challenging conventional gender roles are Vicki's sister and her partner, who are equal participants in a successful business and personal relationship.

Social identity

Vicki's mother cultivates an upper-class identity which requires an ostentatious display of wealth and status; she has closets full of mink (pp.45–6), hundreds of pairs of designer shoes (p.52) and some extremely expensive artworks (p.113). Vicki's mother's need for status symbols, and her arrogant displays of superiority, suggest the emptiness of a life devoid of fulfilling personal relationships.

By contrast, Vicki's sister defines herself as a 'working class' woman because she has 'a job' (p.186). She insists that she lives in a working class suburb, despite the fact that her neighbours have 'two cars and an RV parked in the drive' (p.186). Vicki points out that Gina Rinehart – a wealthy woman who chairs an Australian mining company – also works, but could never be described as working class, and she reminds her sister of their own 'violently aspirational, upper-middle-class background' (p.186). Vicki's sister's stubborn identification with the working class is a rejection of her background, and of the bourgeoise values of the parents who disinherited her. In working to establish her own successful business she feels not only justified in calling herself working class, but proud to do so.

Ageing and identity

In cultures where discrimination on the basis of gender, class, race and age occurs, the elderly are often patronised or treated as social outcasts. Indeed, Vicki hears of one family driving their 'recalcitrant' elderly father to a 'facility in the country' and leaving him there (p.134). Vicki and her sister's experience of caring for their father exposes the chronic mistreatment and neglect of the elderly. Their father's various carers are described by Vicki as a 'housekeeping slut', a 'nymphomaniac', a 'gold-digger', a 'serial killer' and a 'drug addict', all of whom are incapable of holding down a 'mainstream' job (pp.138–9). The delegation of care for the elderly, often to unsuitable and otherwise unemployable people, is a further indication of their unimportance in a ruthless, discriminatory society.

Visiting her mother in hospital, Vicki notes that the nurses are not to be seen, although their heads come forward like 'turtles'' when they hear she is a 'famous author' (p.19). Likewise, in her father's aged-care facility, the staff are 'invisible' and allegedly 'holed up on the nurses' station, texting' (pp.207–8). In the light of such demeaning treatment of the elderly, Vicki's mother's vicious assault on the helpful librarian who drives her to the bank (pp.111–12) can also be viewed as a forceful rejection of assumptions about the infirmity of old age.

National identity

National identity describes a nation as whole, with its distinctive traditions, culture and language. In this memoir, the most visible inhabitants of the region of Canada where Vicki and her sister grew up are descendants of white colonisers, while First Nations people largely exist in the gaps and silences in the narrative. When Vicki and her family attend the annual Calgary Stampede and Rodeo, where men wear 'chaps and Stetsons' and Vicki and her sister dress as 'cowgirls' (p.121), what they unknowingly celebrate is the dispossession of Canada's First Nations peoples.

Particularly problematic at the Stampede is the token presence of First Nations people as a kind of fairground sideshow, although such entertainments were deemed normal at the time. Vicki and her sister are not allowed to visit the 'Indian Village' or to 'go anywhere near any member of the First Nations', but are 'de-loused' when they get home, 'just in case' (p.121). Vicki suggests that her sister might have sought to make amends for her part in her family's ritual: one that she later sees as demeaning to First Nations people. Vicki refers to her sister's adoption of two 'Cree children' (p.121) which might be viewed as a small gesture of recompense for the dispossession of First Nations peoples by her colonising ancestors.

An acknowledgement of the historical mistreatment of First Nations peoples might also be read into Laveau-Harvie's use of Blackfoot mythology in the final section of the memoir (pp.215–17). However, when viewed through a twenty-first-century lens of historical racial prejudice it might, like the Indian Village at the Stampede, be viewed as unacceptable cultural appropriation.

Key point

Vicki's Canadian heritage involves having a traditional '14-foot Douglas fir ... baubles and candy canes and gingerbread Santas' (p.58) to celebrate Christmas, but she is also missing 'mangoes and platters of prawns' and 'photos in the paper of boozed-up Brits on Bondi beach' (p.58). With a heritage divided between Canada and Australia, Vicki is able to bridge the two nations, and identify equally (and in positive ways) with both cultures.

Environment and landscapes

Key quotes

'... I see the Rockies. They shine, lit from behind where the sun has set.' (p.31)
'... the jagged blades of rock that thrust upwards toward us, too steep for snow to cling to, slate-grey, angled and dark.' (p.119)

Environmental degradation

When visiting her sister in Vancouver, Vicki enjoys the 'cascades of fairy lights', illuminated reindeer and 'motion-sensor Santas', but worries about the environmental consequence of this. She thinks of the 'huge greenhouses for strawberries' with 'millions of electric bulbs burning 24 hours a day', and 'for once' is 'glad' that 'Canadians don't understand the conservation of energy' (p.63) – implying that, although at this moment she is enjoying the Christmas lights, her overall view of such wasteful energy use is critical. Although 'hydro energy' seems on the surface to be sustainable, the unasked 'bigger questions' she refers to might be about the consequences of blocking rivers with dams and the degradation of water quality and aquatic habitat.

The catastrophic effects of global warming are also noted on Vicki's 'last trip' to her parents' house 'on the edge of the foothills' (p.169). Vicki is 'braced for the shock of seeing whole slopes of fir trees yellow and dying, victims of the Japanese beetle' which was once killed by 'the brutal cold of a normal winter' but now is able to survive to 'kill its host in the spring' (p.170). Also mentioned as part of the environmental assault is Vicki's mother's vast collection of mink coats (pp.45–6). As Canada's most valuable fur-bearers, almost 34 000 mink were trapped in 1993 and 1994.

The shameful exploitation and depletion of Canada's natural resources is also evident in Vicki's references to the oil wells that 'came roaring in during the boom' of the mid-1940s to the 1980s (p.107). These are places where Vicki's father has worked. He became so wealthy from his work for 'a big oil company' and later from his own 'petroleum consultancy firm' (p.198) that he could consider purchasing the entire Pacific Peace complex (p.189).

Sam Livingston, commemorated in the bronze statue at Calgary airport, exemplifies the colonialist pioneering spirit of the late 1800s that, even until relatively recent times, seemed entirely admirable. After gold prospecting and 'trading in buffalo hides' he 'set his mind to cultivating the rich prairie soil' (inhabited by the Blackfoot Confederacy); he brought the 'first mechanised farm equipment to Calgary, the first threshers and binders' (p.118). He proudly showed visiting British royalty around 'Southern Alberta's innovative agricultural landscape' (pp.118–19), while dispossessed Blackfoot people were gradually moved to reservations.

Environmental protection

Along the highway Vicki imagines her mother's spirit on the edge of the boulder known as the Okotoks Erratic. When Napi, the 'spirit Wise Man of the Blackfoot people', appears, and the spirit of Vicki's mother apologises for her mink hat, he praises her care for animals on the property as well as her daughters' support for environmental initiatives (pp.215–16). The apology from the spirit of a woman who owned closets full of mink (p.45), and the forgiving spirit of a Blackfoot Wise Man, encourage the imagining of greater environmental awareness in modern Canada, and the acknowledgement of First Nations people's respect for the land.

Rocky Mountains landscapes

Dominating the landscape in Southern Alberta are the majestic Rocky Mountains. In spring and summer, they are benign and beautiful:

> Summer glides into fall. The leaves turn and the asters bloom. The Canada geese fly south over the foothills in impeccable V-formation, high, high up in the perfect dome of blue, safe until they land. Along the Sheep River, the walking paths are paved with the gold of the aspen leaves, floating down on the warmth of the Indian-summer sun. (p.115)

The Rockies have a nurturing, spiritual presence as well. At her parents' house, looking out the window Vicki imagines the 'water witch with his forked branch who surveyed the place' when her parents moved there, and who 'missed this hidden stream behind the house' which nourished the giant Douglas fir that her mother planted too close to the house decades earlier (p.42). With their extremes of splendour and menace, the Rockies exert their magnetic power over the people from the prairie who sometimes consider moving to the coast to escape the cold and snow. After visiting the coast, however, they hurry back over the mountains, unable to breathe in the clammy, low altitude, coastal air (p.63).

Sometimes, though, the Rockies have a more sinister presence. In the darkness of winter, the landscape is battered by 'snowfall and blizzard gales' (p.174). Flying above the Rockies, on a plane to Vancouver in winter, Vicki notices the 'jagged blades ... that thrust upwards ... slate-grey, angled and dark', and she thinks of a 'disobedient air-pocket' waiting to plunge their 'airborne sardine tin' onto the mountain and scatter the passengers 'into the chasms below' (p.119).

Even the roads traversing the Rockies and their foothills are perilous. Driving to Shawnessy on Highway 2 with her father, Vicki knows she is in imminent danger of becoming 'part of a prairie apocalypse of overturned semis with their wheels spinning silently in the pale autumn sunlight' (p.100). The Calgary paper's daily stories of 'horrors' on the notorious Banff Highway include 'unbelievable and tragic car accident stories' in which the local paramedics recognise the children they find in 'crumpled' wrecks (p.115). These gruesome details intensify the aura of danger pervading the Rockies' landscapes.

Key point

Traumatic incidents, real and imagined, give the Rockies a powerful and menacing presence in the lives of the people who live in the mountains' shadow, although this is balanced by their beauty and their majesty. It is the view of the Rockies from the window of her parents' house, which her mother 'will never see again' (p.157), that triggers Vicki's grief over her mother's lost battle to return home.

Storytelling

Key quotes

'… I feel differently about Mum's story now that the last page has been written … Dad should be allowed to feel this too.' (p.211)

'And were you even listening to the story about my cloak? It's about not taking back what you have given.' (Napi the Trickster, p.216)

Lies

Vicki's mother is a continual and a compulsive liar. At the hospital, her lie about having 'only … one daughter' who 'died a long time ago' is contradicted by another of her lies, that she had 'eighteen kids' (p.3). Although both lies are relatively trivial, they show that she is utterly unconstrained by the moral values that apply to ordinary people. Other lies are spiteful and hurtful, like the one she tells her husband about Vicki having 'decreed' that they are both to be placed 'into care' (p.146), while the story she tells her doctor about hiding 'old Jews' during World War II (p.148) is cunning and deceitful.

The lies Vicki's mother tells sometimes seem plausible, like the assertion that 'Victoire is so fond of Henry James', although Vicki corrects any false impressions the reader may have formed – 'I have not met him yet, and I won't like him when I do' (p.16). Her mother's 'death' (p.130), seemingly confirmed by the publication of her obituary, *appears* valid (at least to the university human resources department and Vicki's distressed friend): this is because the real truth is entirely unimaginable. On the other hand, the unlikely story about saving old Jews during the war and accounts of her 'fabulous life' and enormous wealth (p.157) are more like escapist fantasies about the person she would like to have been. These inventions are credible to the doctors caught within her 'magic web' (p.149). As is the case with pathological liars, Vicki's mother's stories 'make sense to her' (p.157) and make her the star of her own fantasy world. They also increase her power to manipulate people for her own devious purposes.

Recollections and yarns

When Vicki encourages her father to tell her his stories again, she allows him to slip comfortably back into the world of his youthful adventures, flying in 'single-engine planes over the jungle ... being spirited out the back door of bodegas' and carrying out heroic rescues of 'important and influential women' (p.198). Unlike his wife's lies, which are motivated primarily by self-interest, Vicki's father's stories are a means of sharing and of reinforcing connections. They not only take him back to his adventurous past, but also allow him to settle back and 'yarn' after dinner: to 'embellish', and – just as people have always done – to tell 'stories of who we are or who we think we are' (p.199).

Vicki's father's reminiscences are part of the rich storytelling tradition observed 'around fires in caves ... and over lavish place-settings at gala fundraisers' (p.199); Vicki also understands that retelling his stories enables her father to transcend the alarming circumstances of his 'downward slide' (p.206). In sharing with her Australian family her own story about her Canadian heritage and the complexities of her family background, Vicki leaves them an important legacy to hand down to future generations. Moreover, her reassessment of her mother's story after her death suggests that the writing of one's life experiences – especially painful ones – can help to heal.

Newspaper articles

The Calgary daily paper runs stories about damage and destruction: 'seals are blown out of the water off Alaska by American weapons testing', cats are stuck up trees and babies have 'their heads stuck in railings'. 'Four dead', Vicki's sister mutters one morning, passing her in the hall (p.115). It is this 'gallery of horrors' that Vicki's mother eagerly shares with her family for their 'edification' at the breakfast table each morning. Given her damaging and destructive behaviour, her focus on everyday violence in the world might make her own harmful actions seem like 'the new normal' (p.127).

Myths

Mythical accounts of heroes and celebrations of significant events connect people with stories of their beginnings, or unite them within a group whose stories they share. Myths also ensure the preservation of unique cultural identities through rituals (such as Christmas festivities or the Calgary Stampede) for which there are 'deep cultural reasons' (p.57), and which are expressed in the public display of symbolic objects such as 'fairy lights' (p.63) and cowgirl costumes (p.121).

A sense of mystery and a promise of spiritual guidance makes certain myths very powerful. The story told by Napi is compelling in this sense: it is the story of the giving of his cloak as a token of gratitude to the Okotok rock for its hospitality when he needed rest, but also of its revenge when he takes back his gift (pp.215–16). The values endorsed by this myth are respect for the natural world, and the need to honour the giving of a gift.

Key point

Wearing her ankle-length black mink coat and matching hat, the spirit of Vicki's mother apologises to Napi (p.215), whose story reminds her that what has been given cannot be taken back, and reassures her that 'we do what we can' (p.216). This seems to suggest acceptance of the past and hope for the future.

Family

Key quotes

'There would be no polite questions about the length of my trip or about how many children I might have now.' (p.96)

'She is my sister and I care about her. She's sick. She is my link to my father. I listen.' (p.203)

Since the middle of the twentieth century, different ways of being a 'family' have emerged. As well as comprising married couples with one or more children, family groups might now consist of single parents, same-sex relationships, childless couples and blended families. Most of these are represented in Laveau-Harvie's memoir, and seemingly act in ways that affirm 'family values': responsible adults care for and support each other; safe environments are created for children and suitable moral values are promoted. In the nuclear family of Vicki's childhood, it is the complete absence of these values that define her dysfunctional family.

Traditional nuclear families

There are glaring differences between Vicki's dysfunctional family and the close-knit family of her uncle and aunt, whose perspectives widen 'with each new baby, blossoming like ... paper flower buds that unfold into unexpected beauty' (p.86), their lives abundant with 'Hallmark moments' (p.32). Vicki's own Australian family includes her (former) husband (p.182), her daughter (p.80) and her son who lives in Hong Kong (p.71). Her relationships with her children are sufficiently close that she can share with them some of what she feels about her parents, although neither her son nor her daughter have a connection with their maternal grandparents.

Blended family

Vicki is invited to Christmas dinner with her sister and her sister's partner at the home of 'newlywed second-timers' (p.64). The wife's teenage daughter leaves at the end of the meal to see her '"real" dad' who apparently has to work hard 'just keeping it real' (p.64). Vicki is grateful to these people for having 'their own problems' (p.64) and for giving her the chance to reflect on the everyday 'dangers and difficulties' people must deal with (p.65). Yet Vicki's idealised view of family life is coloured by the aura of happiness surrounding her uncle and aunt's family; this might make blended family structures seem problematic and lead her to imagine that the 'real' father is 'maybe chronically late with child-support payments' (p.64). Nevertheless, this blended family shows Vicki that 'confronting the real makes you a person of substance' (p.65).

Partnerships

As a cohabiting couple in a business partnership, Vicki's sister and her partner are a successful family. They 'shoulder almost all of what needs doing' (p.135) for Vicki's sister's parents: they offer to build a house closer to the family home (p.74) and enlist friends to help tackle the dangerous, exhausting task of clearing years of accumulated rubbish out of the house (pp.178–9). The calm practicality shown by Vicki's sister's partner at the hospital (p.194) is a buffer against her sister's tendency to be overemotional and uncompromising. That their relationship succeeds can be seen as a reflection of the spirit of cooperation and equality embedded in the idea of a 'partnership'.

Siblings

As they discover when Vicki babysits her sister as a child, their own positive views of themselves are sometimes seen by each other as character flaws (p.129), and an element of tension lingers in their adult relationship. When Vicki returns to Canada, they disagree on strategies for dealing with their mother and her sister accepts Vicki's 'win' with 'bad grace' (p.11), suggesting a degree of sibling rivalry in their (mostly) supportive sisterly relationship. Nevertheless, the challenges they face also bring them closer as they laugh and cry together over their father's embarrassingly inappropriate language about his manly attributes (p.200).

Parents

Ageing parents, and the challenges of coping with them, are a focal point in the memoir. Vicki's parents are well cared for, but other aged parents are sometimes treated like 'unwanted pets' (p.134). A tragic example is the 'recalcitrant' old man whose family abandons him in a remote facility in the country. Also cruelly forsaken is the lady resident in the Pacific Peace complex. Wearing 'pantsuits and … pearls', she lies 'stiffly' on the bed 'so that she won't crease her outfit' and waits patiently (like most residents there) for 'people who never come' (p.207).

Examples like these highlight the distress and frustration often felt by families of elderly and infirm parents, and also suggest the breakdown of close-knit family and community networks with supportive neighbours. On the other hand, the text also portrays individuals such as those who rally around Vicki's father after the burglary (pp.66–7). These people are exceptional in their neighbourly support. Some have experienced 'the sadness of having to put a loved one into care' (p.55) and they become willingly involved in a community network of care for Vicki's father, which enables him to remain in his home.

DIFFERENT INTERPRETATIONS

Different interpretations arise from differing responses to a text. Over time, a text will evoke a wide range of responses from its readers, who may come from various social or cultural groups and live in very different places and historical periods. Responses by critics and reviewers can be published in newspapers, journals and books, both online and in print. They can also be expressed in discussions among readers in the media, classrooms, book groups and so on.

While there is no single correct reading or interpretation of a text, it is important to understand that an interpretation is more than a personal opinion – it is the justification of a point of view on the text. To present an interpretation of a text based on your point of view, you must use a logical argument and support it with relevant evidence from the text.

Critical viewpoints

The Erratics has been well received by critics, and the various reviewers who have praised the book have tended to focus on different aspects of it.

Melissa Thorne, a literary critic, writes for a well-read audience in the *Sydney Review of Books*. She draws particular attention to Laveau-Harvie's descriptions of landscape, quoting a comment by Laveau-Harvie herself that the Rockies are 'practically a character in the book'. The 'titular erratics', as Thorne explains, 'are Laveau-Harvie's family' (Thorne 2019). Further developing the metaphor, Thorne asserts that 'Laveau-Harvie herself is erratic, wandering to distant continents to survive and stay sane'. She cites Laveau-Harvie's reading notes, in which the author describes her mother as 'the very definition of unreliability, unpredictability, ominous disorder'. The memoir, Thorne explains, examines Laveau-Harvie's mother's 'legacy' of 'chaos', pointing out that 'the other prominent erratic ... is the Okotoks Erratic, a huge boulder deposited by glacial flow thousands of years ago which cracked and "fell in on itself"'. The connection between the rock and Vicki's mother emphasises the destructive potential of each of them.

Jenny Valentish, in her review for *The Guardian*, focuses on Laveau-Harvie's depiction of family relationships. She provides background details such as the author's eighteen-year estrangement from her parents, and emphasises Vicki's mother's bizarre and destructive behaviour:

> When she was growing up, legions of friends and neighbours were ostracised by her mother, further and further isolating the family. Her mother repeatedly regarded the girls with a strange kind of sorrow, observing, "I'll get you and you won't even know I'm doing it." Once, she cut off Laveau-Harvie's ponytail with sewing shears in a fit of spite. (Valentish 2019)

While listening to Laveau-Harvie's interview with Richard Fidler on ABC Radio's *Conversations*, Valentish had thought the book 'sounded like a misery memoir'. However, she decided after reading it that Laveau-Harvie's 'agile humour – albeit of the gallows variety – transforms it into something quite of its own genre', mitigating the effects of depicting cruelty and trauma through a deft use of style and tone, and 'moments of tenderness springing up like flowers in a melting snowscape'.

Professional reviews aren't the only form of published interpretation. Online bloggers can provide book reviews, and these may be open to reader comments, as in the case of the blog 'Whispering Gums', self-described as a discussion forum for 'books, reading and anything else that comes to mind ... with an Australian focus'. In a 2019 review of *The Erratics*, the blogger (whisperinggums) writes that there is something disquieting about Laveau-Harvie's tone. While admiring Laveau-Harvie's 'fearless honesty' and comparing her with Helen Garner, who is 'not afraid to say the hard, unpalatable things', whisperinggums found Laveau-Harvie's memoir 'difficult at times' because 'this "honesty" was attended by an unkindness, by a willingness to laugh at another's expense', though the reviewer concedes that Laveau-Harvie also frequently laughs at her own expense.

In explaining what they find 'disquieting' the blogger cites Laveau-Harvie's description of 'the array of carers she and her sister put in place for their father'. While admitting that this is 'funny, and has an element of truth, recognisable by anyone who has experienced the situation', the blogger dislikes 'name-calling' and thus does not think the author's references to 'the gold-digger' and 'the housekeeping slut' are funny.

Two interpretations of *The Erratics*

Interpretation 1: *The Erratics* is a deeply pessimistic story about death, decay and destruction.

Vicki Laveau-Harvie's memoir is a dismal narrative about her highly dysfunctional family. As children, Vicki and her sister are neglected and terrorised by their mother, who also dominates her husband, a benign but ineffectual father. Moreover, the unpleasant details of Vicki's parents' physical and mental decline are exceedingly depressing. Even though there are some darkly humorous moments, an atmosphere of gloom pervades the narrative.

Many of Vicki's childhood experiences are so disturbing that they are replaced by blank spaces in her memory. After her mother suddenly and brutally shears off her ponytail, Vicki remembers only the 'cold metal' on the back of her head and the 'crisp whisper of the blades closing'; of the 'aftermath' she remembers 'nothing' (p.122). Vicki's sister remembers vividly, but supresses her 'rage' (p.35). Beneath her impassive surface her anger simmers like a 'geyser' waiting to erupt 'suddenly, shockingly', turning everything 'black and viscous … as it falls to earth' (p.35), and years later, passing a girl with a ponytail in the street still makes her shudder. Laveau-Harvie's warning about the damaging long-term effects of suppressed shock or anger is echoed in a disturbing environmental parallel with the Japanese beetle, now able to survive warmer winters concealed under the bark of fir trees, and to emerge and 'kill its host' in the springtime (p.170). The 'yellow and dying' trees (p.170) are also metaphorically linked with Vicki's sister's almost fatal illness after her contact with toxins in the disused bomb shelter on her parents' property (p.202). These examples of extreme and often irreparable damage are ample cause for pessimism.

Almost unbearably depressing is the memoir's focus on ageing and death. At ninety-four, and still capable of being 'charming and witty' (p.153), Vicki's mother disguises the signs of ageing with her dyed and bobbed black hair, but her 'crumbling' hip (p.126) lands her in hospital. She is eventually diagnosed as 'mentally incompetent' (p.156) and incarcerated in the dementia ward, where her loss of freedom will cause her 'deep pain' (p.134) and 'despair' (p.135).

Equally tragic, and perhaps more moving for the reader, is Vicki's father's decline. Despite humorous moments such as his boastful reference to the size of his penis (p.199), his mental deterioration is painfully obvious: not only is he unable to tell his daughters apart, he cannot even remember their names (p.23). Physically, he declines in 'tiny increments', becoming 'a little slower' and 'a little deafer' and he can feel, as Vicki observes, the 'downward slide' (p.206).

The metaphor of a train journey is particularly gloomy in its reminder that we will all 'complete [the] journey' to the 'end of the line' (p.205), although it is not just the inevitability of death that is so troubling, but the daunting prospect of old age. In her father's aged-care facility, the staff 'are invisible', and residents wait in vain for 'people who never come' (p.207). This suggests a widespread lack of concern and compassion for the elderly in contemporary Western societies. Even more distressing are stories of elderly parents who are callously abandoned in remote care facilities by families who consider them a nuisance.

Yet it is not only the elderly for whom death is 'the end of the line' (p.205); it can strike at any time, swiftly and shockingly, reminding us of the precariousness of existence. The Calgary newspaper's 'gallery of horrors', to which Vicki's mother subjects her family each morning (p.115), suggests that similar horrors await the unwary population, while her dire warning of dangerous intruders lurking at the door with the intention of doing harm portrays the outside world as a very frightening place (p.128). Vicki's exposure to such a pessimistic view explains her tendency to contemplate her own sudden and violent death: flying to Hong Kong, she imagines her plane crashing and scattering the passengers among the Rockies' 'jagged' peaks (p.119). On the road to Shawnessy, she pictures herself in a 'prairie apocalypse' of overturned semitrailers, and then becoming 'a paragraph in the *Okotoks Chronicle*' (pp.99–100). These gruesome imaginings are also a consequence of living in the shadow of the Rockies where a sudden rockslide on an unstable slope once killed scores of people (p.10). Also vivid in Vicki's memory is the fire that burned down the centre of the town of Black Diamond, where she lived as a child (p.107).

Whether death is a peaceful conclusion to life, as Vicki's mother's death is, or an abrupt extinction on a highway, there is little doubt that the memoir's emphasis on death and destruction creates a pervasive atmosphere of gloom. Ageing is also shown as a sad deterioration of the mind and the body and is, as Laveau-Harvie's metaphor of the train journey emphasises, an unavoidable fact of our existence. Despite fleeting moments of happiness, it seems there is little to celebrate in the lives of Vicki's family.

Interpretation 2: Humour and optimism make *The Erratics* an inspiring story.

On the surface, *The Erratics* seems to be an unremittingly bleak account of ageing and death. Its horror stories about rockslides, road fatalities, explosions and fires suggest the fragility of human life in the face of disasters, both natural and caused by human activity. Despite this, Vicki finds much to be positive and joyful about. Her reconnection with her Canadian family after an absence of eighteen years is – apart from contact with her mother – a positive experience and, unexpectedly, she gains a more optimistic view of her mother.

Vicki's guilt over her sister's burden of care for their ageing parents has cast a shadow over their relationship, yet their bond is strengthened as they join forces to ensure that their mother never returns home to 'finish ... off' (p.33) their father. As they clean their parents' house there are moments of black humour, such as the carer's suggestion of 'carbon dating' items in the fridge (p.22) and their father's sudden recollection of his suppositories, prompted by Vicki's reference to the 'bottom-line' (p.40). This impulse to find humour in distressing circumstances shows resilience and a determination not to be defeated.

Dealing with their mother brings different challenges, which the sisters face together. After searching their mother's closets for suitable hospital clothing, Vicki and her sister look out the window of their mother's room and Vicki's sister squeezes her hand (p.52). This poignant moment of sisterly solidarity and affection softens their occasionally 'unfriendly' (p.41) interactions. Vicki also reunites with her uncle and aunt, a loving couple with a large and happy family (p.86). Their efforts to welcome her emphasise the strength of their 'blood' relationships (p.17). On her final day in Alberta, they and their daughter drive Vicki around the towns of her childhood and she is overwhelmed by their kindness (p.106).

Also positive is Vicki's reconnection with her father. Although previously convinced by his wife that his daughters are only after their parents' money, and consenting to disinherit them and banish them from his life (p.187), he recovers from her brainwashing and her attempts to starve him to death, gratefully acknowledging 'all that you girls do for me' (p.167). This is an encouraging sign that even very damaged family relationships can be salvaged.

Another cause for optimism is the spirited resilience of Gerta in the aged-care facility. Allegedly sent there 'under severe duress', she is a forceful presence and fills the 'void' in Vicki's father's life (p.189). A different kind of void is the burnt-out town of Black Diamond, where useful buildings from 'ghost towns' are retrieved and sent to 'serve again' (p.108). This suggests that a traumatic past can be a repository for things of value, such as the rocking horse made for Vicki's father by Air Force friends when Vicki was born, which she salvages for her granddaughter. Black Diamond also unlocks a comforting memory: she is scooped up and held close by a stranger who turns out to be her father, back home after a long absence. As he carries her into the house she feels safe (p.107) and it seems both fitting and heartening that as an adult she is now able to help her father to be safe.

Further positive signs in the face of impending disaster are the small steps taken to protect the environment. Vicki and her sister fundraise for the Pacific Whale Foundation and sign petitions against shark culling and live animal exports (p.217); Vicki's father is involved in an environmental campaign for clean water (p.19), and her mother protected animals on her property and treated them with respect – ironically something she could not do for her family. The efforts of these environmental protection groups provide a spark of hope that a 'downward slide' towards environmental unsustainability might gradually be slowed.

The care and concern shown by environmentalists are echoed in the strong sense of community responsibility evident when neighbours arrive at Vicki's father's house after the attempted burglary, bringing 'sheets of plywood' to repair the broken windows, and laden with plates of Christmas 'leftovers' (p.67). This is despite the damage caused by Vicki's mother, whose previous hostile interactions with the neighbours have left their 'stamp' (p.55). Not the least of the optimistic elements of the memoir is Vicki's admission that she feels 'differently' about her mother's story 'now that the last page has been written' (p.211). Her mother's utterance of the word 'sorry' when she apologises to Napi about the 'farmed mink' (p.215) might equally apply to other things she regrets.

There is much cause for optimism in Vicki Laveau-Harvie's account of her very dysfunctional family. Beneath the damage caused by her mother's malevolence is the notion that 'blood calls to blood' and that, along with environmental sustainability, family relationships are what matter most. Given that these relationships are so badly damaged, yet seem – at least in most cases – to be repairable, *The Erratics* can be seen as an uplifting story of reconciliation.

QUESTIONS & ANSWERS

This section focuses on your own analytical writing on the text, and gives you strategies for producing high-quality responses in your coursework and exam essays.

Essay writing – an overview

An essay on a literary work is a formal and serious piece of writing that presents your point of view on the text, usually in response to a given topic. Your 'point of view' in an essay is your interpretation of the meaning of the text's language, structure, characters, situations and events, supported by detailed analysis of textual evidence.

Analyse – don't summarise

In your essays it is important to avoid simply summarising what happens in a text.

- A **summary** is a description or paraphrase (retelling in different words) of the characters and events. For example: 'Macbeth has a horrifying vision of a dagger dripping with blood before he goes to murder King Duncan.'
- An **analysis** is an explanation of the real meaning or significance that lies 'beneath' the text's words (and images, for a film). For example: 'Macbeth's vision of a bloody dagger shows how deeply uneasy he is about the violent act he is contemplating, and conveys his sense that supernatural forces are impelling him to act.'

A limited amount of summary is sometimes necessary to let your reader know which part of the text you wish to discuss. However, always keep this to a minimum and follow it immediately with your analysis of what this part of the text is really telling us.

Plan your essay

Carefully plan your essay so that you have a clear idea of what you are going to say. The plan ensures that your ideas flow logically, that your argument remains consistent and that you stay on the topic. An essay plan should be a list of **brief dot points** covering no more than half a page.

- Include your central argument or main contention – a concise statement of your overall response to the topic.
- Write three or four dot points for each paragraph, indicating the main idea and evidence/examples from the text. Note that in your essay you will need to *expand* on these points and *analyse* the evidence.

Structure your essay

An essay is a complete, self-contained piece of writing. It has a clear beginning (the introduction), middle (several body paragraphs) and end (the last paragraph or conclusion). It must also have a central argument that runs throughout, linking each paragraph to form a coherent whole. See examples of introductions and conclusions in the 'Analysing a sample topic' and 'Sample answer' sections.

The introduction establishes your overall response to the topic. It includes your main contention and outlines the main evidence you will refer to in the course of the essay. Write your introduction *after* you have done a plan and *before* you write the rest of the essay.

The body paragraphs argue your case – they present evidence from the text and explain how this evidence supports your argument. Each body paragraph needs:

- a strong topic **sentence** (usually the first sentence) that states the main point being made in the paragraph
- **evidence** from the text, including some brief quotations
- **analysis** of the textual evidence, with **explanation** of its significance and how it supports your argument

- **links back to the topic** in one or more statements, usually towards the end of the paragraph.

Connect the body paragraphs so that your discussion flows smoothly. Use some linking words and phrases such as 'similarly' and 'on the other hand', though don't start every paragraph like this. Another strategy is to use a significant word from the last sentence of one paragraph in the first sentence of the next.

Use key terms from the topic – or synonyms for them – throughout, so the relevance of your discussion to the topic is always clear.

The conclusion ties everything together and finishes the essay. It includes strong statements that emphasise your central argument and provide a clear response to the topic.

Avoid simply restating the points made earlier in the essay – this will end on a very flat note and imply that you have run out of ideas and vocabulary. The conclusion should be a logical extension of what you have written, not just a repetition or summary of it. Writing an effective conclusion can be a challenge. Try using these tips:

- Start by linking back to the final sentence of the second-last paragraph, rather than leaping to your main contention straight away – this helps your writing to flow.
- Use synonyms and expressions with equivalent meanings to vary your vocabulary. This allows you to reinforce your line of argument without being repetitive.
- When planning your essay, think of one or two broad statements or observations about the text's wider meaning. These should be related to the topic and your overall argument. Keep them for the conclusion, since they will give you something 'new' to say but still follow logically from your discussion. The introduction will be focused on the topic, but the conclusion can present a wider view of the text.

Essay topics

1. "… she squeezes my hand and we stand together like that, looking out the window …"
   How is the unsettled relationship between Vicki and her sister repaired as they cope with their difficult family circumstances?
2. "My past is not merely faded … It's not there."
   How do the events of the past shape the lives of the individuals in *The Erratics*?
3. 'Vicki's mother is the most destructive presence in *The Erratics*.'
   Do you agree?
4. 'Family is the most powerful influence on the individuals in this text.'
   To what extent do you agree?
5. "She has her truth and I have mine …"
   How is the idea of truth explored in *The Erratics*?
6. How important are communities to the individuals in *The Erratics*?
7. How does Laveau-Harvie show the importance of home in *The Erratics*?
8. "… to tell the stories of who we are or who we think we are."
   What role does storytelling play in *The Erratics*?
9. How does *The Erratics* explore ideas about power?
10. '*The Erratics* is a disturbing account of how conflicting values can fracture relationships.' Discuss.

Vocabulary for writing on *The Erratics*

Characterisation: Aspects of character are conveyed through actions, relationships and dialogue. Connections between aspects of character and other elements of a text, such as features of the Rockies in *The Erratics*, are also revealing.

Imagery: A form of figurative language, imagery includes similes, metaphors and sensory images (mainly visual in *The Erratics*). For example, Vicki's simile describing herself as a wonton wrapper (p.45) suggests her emotional fragility and implies a sense of disconnection from the land of her birth.

Irony: Irony is an important element of style in *The Erratics*. An example of **verbal irony** can be found in the account of Vicki's evening meal with her parents, in her ironic assertion that 'to say that the dinner-table conversation was stilted would be to accord it a grace and spontaneity it lacked' (p.96). The language and tone are restrained and lighthearted, as if the situation was merely slightly awkward, but the reader knows, from the subsequent details (Vicki's mother 'was clearly not going to acknowledge [her] in any way'), that it must have been agonisingly painful, so the tone here is one of ironic understatement. Laveau-Harvie also uses **situational irony**, for instance when she is alarmed by her father's erratic driving on a dangerous highway *and* leaves her seatbelt unfastened, yet both arrive safely (as the reader knows they must) in Shawnessy.

Motif: A motif is a theme or recurring idea in a text. In *The Erratics*, themes include relationships, ageing, truth and storytelling. The Rockies could also be seen as a motif. In your analysis, references to a motif indicate an awareness of the text as a literary construct.

Narrative point of view: Because a memoir is narrated from the writer's point of view, readers' ways of understanding events and individuals are shaped by the writer's perceptions. Vicki is a reliable narrator in the sense that she endeavours to be honest; her credibility is enhanced by her admission that her sister's version of the truth differs from hers, and also by her recognition that sometimes she gets things 'wrong' (p.109).

Setting: Discussions of setting should recognise subtle connections between physical spaces and the people who inhabit them. For example, Vicki's son, who can 'wizard chaos into fun' (p.71), seems to belong in the 'razzle and the dazzle of the jazziest harbour in the world' (p.70).

Symbol: The many symbols in the text, such as the Rockies and the Erratics, provide scope for thoughtful discussions of meaning. For example, Peabody, the abandoned peacock (pp.74–5), represents both the sad fate of many elderly parents considered troublesome, and also Vicki's father's stubborn endurance of his suffering.

Analysing a sample topic

'*The Erratics* is a disturbing account of how conflicting values can fracture relationships.' Discuss.

The introduction should be a response to your interrogation of the topic. Ask yourself questions such as the following:

- Do you agree with the topic assertion?
- Which word/s in the topic might need a brief explanation?
- Which values might be relevant to a discussion of the topic?
- What are some ways that relationships can be fractured?

Sample introduction

> *The Erratics* examines fractured relationships in families and among social and cultural groups. In a competitive society, the powerful are in control and their values are often driven by self-interest. Vicki's family acts as a microcosm of such a society, and the harmful effects of conflicts between the desire for power on the one hand, and the desire for peace and harmony on the other, are evident. All the relationships in this family are fractured, and not all can recover. However, Vicki and her sister share values such as equality, loyalty and respect, and by working together they are able to strengthen at least some family ties and peacefully resolve conflicts.

Body paragraph outline

Paragraph 1: Conflicting values are the cause of fragmented relationships in Vicki's family.

- Driven by spite and her mercenary values, Vicki's mother convinces her husband to banish and disinherit their daughters whom she alleges are 'just after the money' (p.79). Vicki and her sister cannot forget that their father 'went along' with this (p.188) and become distressed and resentful.
- Vicki's father's 'love' (p.33) for his wife overrides his fatherly responsibility to his daughters, whose names he forgets (p.23), and outweighs his loyalty to his brother (p.79), contributing to the deterioration of the family.
- The importance of her own freedom and safety takes Vicki to 'far-flung places' (p.120), but conflicts with the value that her sister places on family responsibility, and unsettles the relationship between the sisters. Vicki is weighed down by a burden of 'guilt' (p.136) and tensions simmer between the sisters (p.188).
- By contrast, the close and mutually supportive relationship between Vicki's sister and her partner is based on respect and equal sharing of family and work responsibilities (p.165).

Paragraph 2: Disrespect for the values of others also causes disharmony in communities.

- Vicki's mother's hostile behaviour shows complete disrespect for the values of honesty, trust and respect commonly held by other people. Her vicious physical and verbal attacks upset neighbours (p.55), tradesmen (p.165) and unsuspecting members of the public (p.112).
- Disrespect for the rights of the elderly devalues them as human beings. Society's apparent lack of concern over this is an implicit endorsement of discriminatory values (p.134, p.189).
- At the Calgary Stampede, First Nations people are demeaned by the self-interest and assumed racial superiority of colonisers (p.121). The damage to their culture seems irreparable.

Paragraph 3: While acknowledging the harm caused by conflicting values, Vicki is also comforted by harmonious family and social networks, and she endorses the respectful values they represent.

- Vicki and her sister's strong bond of family loyalty is embedded in the idea that 'blood calls to blood' (p.17). Their commitment to their father's welfare is repaid by his gratitude for everything they do for him (p.167) and their fractured relationship is repaired.
- Family loyalty is also important to Vicki's warm-hearted uncle and aunt, who welcome her and care for her on her return to Canada (e.g. pp.86–8). They are a shining exemplar of family values.
- United by the spirit of community responsibility, the neighbourhood rallies around Vicki's father after the attempted burglary, despite the rift caused by Vicki's mother's hostility (p.55).
- Environmental groups demonstrate their commitment to sustainability through campaigns to save endangered species and protect vulnerable ecosystems (p.217).

Sample conclusion

> Conflicting values are at the centre of the fractured relationships in *The Erratics*, where some individuals seek power, wealth and status. Vicki's hostile and acquisitive mother is the embodiment of these values, and her relationships with those who do not share her values suffer accordingly. Yet individuals and communities who share the values of decency and compassion, such as Vicki and her sister, or the family of their uncle and aunt, can enable renewal and reconciliation.

SAMPLE ANSWER

'It is the way Laveau-Harvie tells her family's story, not the story itself, that makes *The Erratics* so powerful.' Discuss.

The Erratics is an account of Vicki Laveau-Harvie's family breakdown, caused by the malevolence of her 'bitter' and 'vindictive' mother. Highlighting the horror of Vicki and her sister's childhood are disturbing details of their mother's neglect and cruelty, and the aura of menace she exudes is greatly intensified by Laveau-Harvie's comparisons of her mother's behaviour with the Rockies' capacity for destruction. While the story itself is compelling, what makes it so powerful is Laveau-Harvie's writing, which draws readers into her fractured world.

Vicki and her sister grow up in a Gothic house of horrors, terrorised by a mother who is out to 'get them'. This makes Vicki's sister's reference to their mother as 'the wicked witch' seem entirely appropriate. The girls are entrapped by their social and physical isolation in a nocturnal landscape of 'thick, black' darkness where 'no one can hear you scream'. Returning home as an adult, Vicki finds her father being 'systematically starved'. When her mother 'surges' from a 'dark doorway' to push her violently against the wall, Vicki suddenly realises that her mother might kill her father by pushing him down the stairs. There is also a rifle propped 'in a corner of the study'. The deeply threatening atmosphere created by these details, combined with macabre imagery of Vicki's 'desiccating' father, sitting in a tractor with a 'cadaver's grin on his face', draws on the themes and imagery of Gothic fiction – a genre that tells stories of helpless victims trapped in isolated and gloomy environments, where they are slowly tortured and brutally killed. Laveau-Harvie's Gothic imagery places her mother's behaviour within a literary tradition that uncovers a dark and sadistic side of human nature.

Adding to the menacing atmosphere are frequent references to hidden dangers and unforeseen fatalities; these establish a symbolic connection with Vicki's mother's hostilities. A cramp in Vicki's foot, possibly deep vein thrombosis, could, without warning, cause Vicki's sudden death, and an allusion to *In Cold Blood*, telling of the murder of an unsuspecting farming family, suggests the possibility of a similar fate for Vicki's family. Most evocative of danger, however, is the imagery of the natural world. Metaphorical connections between the titular 'Erratics' and Vicki's mother make this danger 'palpable' and, just as the Okotoks Erratic 'dominates the landscape', Vicki's mother dominates the narrative. Her capacity for destruction is juxtaposed with the lethal instability of the mountain slope, where a rockslide killed 'scores' of people in the town of Frank. Vicki's mother is also dangerously unpredictable, as the 'unsuspecting' librarian, who is viciously clubbed over the head after offering her assistance, discovers. In a more lethal example of life's dangerous unpredictability, a 'capricious little updraft' over the Rockies might, Vicki imagines, plunge plane-loads of passengers onto the jagged rocks below. Most insidious, however, are Vicki's mother's sadistic schemes, such as the attempt to kill her husband by insisting on the potentially fatal trip to Shawnessy. With three lanes of huge trucks 'screaming' towards them, Vicki imagines becoming part of a 'prairie apocalypse'. The aura of deadly violence emanating from Vicki's mother is often overwhelming.

It is not just graphic images of danger and destruction that bring the writing so vividly to life; there are also glowing descriptions of positive moments. Through their personification, the Rockies can boast of their pleasant valleys: 'look at me all temperate and fertile, you can even grow fruit here'. Also emphasised, through poetic language, is the beauty of the natural world. Returning to her childhood home and family after eighteen years, Vicki is overwhelmed by the breathtaking beauty of the Rockies. Laveau-Harvie's visual imagery is extravagant as she describes the way the mountains are lit by the opalescence of the setting sun, and Vicki admires the 'pearly' band of horizon beneath a 'sapphire' sky, where a star shines 'like a diamond'. This metaphorical connection between the mountain landscape and precious gems suggests their valued place in Vicki's notions of home. These are no ordinary mountains; they are endowed with a spiritual presence, revealed especially through Laveau-Harvie's incorporation of elements of magic realism in the final section of the memoir, embedded in the creation myth told by the spirit Wise Man of the Blackfoot people.

The juxtaposition of Laveau-Harvie's story against the powerful backdrop of Rocky Mountain landscapes creates scope for thought-provoking comparisons. While the dangers of the Rockies and the traumatic events in Vicki's childhood heighten the aura of malevolence, images of beauty and benevolence in the mountain landscapes convey positive notions of nurturing and renewal. Moreover, the skilful incorporation of elements of Gothic fiction and magic realism adds layers of deeper meaning to the text. The memoir's imaginative and often poetic style makes a powerful impression on the reader, particularly in combination with its confronting and moving subject matter.

REFERENCES & READING

Text

Laveau Harvie, V 2019, *The Erratics*, Fourth Estate, Sydney.

References and further reading

Cuddon, JA 1999, *The Penguin Dictionary of Literary Terms & Literary Theory*, Penguin Books, Victoria.

Davidson, R & Smith, P 2021, 'Alberta history', *Encyclopaedia Britannica*, https://www.britannica.com/place/Alberta-province/History

Reviews, articles and interviews

Fidler, R & Laveau-Harvie, V 2018, 'An Erratic Family Saga', *ABC Radio Conversations*, June, https://www.abc.net.au/radio/programs/conversations/vicki-laveau-harvie-rpt/11036454

Judges' Report 2019, https://thestellaprize.com.au/prize/2019-prize/the-erratics/

Laveau-Harvie, V 2019, 'I needed to deal with my destructive demons before I could write about my past', *The Guardian*, 14 May, https://www.theguardian.com/books/2019/may/13/i-needed-to-deal-with-my-destructive-demons-before-i-could-write-about-my-past

Sehgal, P 2020, '*The Erratics* remembers a mother with a monstrous talent for twisting reality', *The New York Times*, 11 August, https://www.nytimes.com/2020/08/11/books/review-erratics-vicki-laveau-harvie.html

The Garrett: Writers on Writing 2019, 'The Stella Prize 2019: Vicki Laveau-Harvie', https://thegarretpodcast.com/vicki-laveau-harvie/

The Stella Interview 2019, https://thestellaprize.com.au/2019/03/stella-interview-vicki-laveau-harvie-erratics/

The Stella Prize Acceptance Speech 2020, https://thestellaprize.com.au/2019/04/vicki-laveau-harvies-2019-stella-prize-acceptance-speech/

Thorne, M 2019, 'Blood Calls to Blood', *Sydney Review of Books*, 24 July, https://sydneyreviewofbooks.com/review/erratics-laveau-harvie

Valentish, J 2019, 'The Unmissables: *The Erratics* by Vicki Laveau-Harvie – a memoir of entirely its own genre', *The Guardian*, 13 May, https://www.theguardian.com/books/2019/may/13/the-unmissables-the-erratics-by-vicki-laveau-harvie-a-memoir-of-entirely-its-own-genre

whisperinggums 2019, 'Vicki Laveau-Harvie, The Erratics (#BookReview)', Whispering Gums, 25 April, https://whisperinggums.com/2019/04/25/vicki-laveau-harvie-the-erratics-bookreview